THE CONCISE GUIDE SERIES

a concise guide to

Your Rights
in the
Catholic
Church

the concise guide series

The Concise Guide Series offers Catholics a deeper understanding of contemporary pastoral issues that directly impact Catholic life and identity today. The series offers Church leaders—whether lay or ordained, paid professionals or well-equipped volunteers—excellent reference guides to the vast complexity of Church teaching that lays the foundation of their ministry. Steeped in loving commitment to the pastoral life of the Church, the books of the Concise Guide Series tackle contemporary pastoral issues and carefully situate them within the structures of Catholic tradition.

A Concise Guide to Canon Law

A Concise Guide to Catholic Social Teaching

A Concise Guide to Your Rights in the Catholic Church

THE CONCISE GUIDE SERIES

a concise guide to

Your Rights in the Catholic Church

Kevin E. McKenna

ave maria press AmP notre dame, indiana

© 2006 by Ave Maria Press, Inc.

Founded in 1865, Ave Maria Press is a ministry of the Indiana Province of Holy Cross.

www.avemariapress.com

ISBN-10 1-59471-079-1 ISBN-13 978-1-59471-079-7

Revised cover design by Andy Wagoner

Text design by Katherine Robinson Coleman

Printed and bound in the United States of America.

Library of Congress Cataloging-in-Publication Data

McKenna, Kevin E., 1950-
  A concise guide to your rights in the Catholic Church / Kevin E.
McKenna.
    p. cm. — (Concise guide series)
  Includes bibliographical references and index.
  ISBN-13: 978-1-59471-079-7 (pbk.)
  ISBN-10: 1-59471-079-1 (pbk.)
    1. Laity (Canon law) 2. Clergy (Canon law) 3. Catholics—Legal
status, laws, etc.   I. Title. II. Series.
  KBU2312.M36 2006
  262.9′4—dc22

                                    2006007819

To Rev. Francis Morrisey, O.M.I.,
in recognition and appreciation of
his tireless efforts to make the rights
of God's people a reality and lived
experience in the Church today.

CONTENTS

6. Vindicating Rights in the Church   *89*

Appendices

This book responds to a question that is being asked by many Catholics today, both clergy and laity: "Do I have rights in the Catholic Church?" And if I do, another question comes immediately to mind: "What are my rights?" These questions have been fueled, to a large extent, by the exploding sexual abuse scandal that has raged throughout the Church in the United States. The report of the John Jay College of Criminal Justice in New York, commissioned by the United States Conference of Catholic Bishops in response to the sexual abuse scandal, revealed that approximately 4,392 clergy allegedly abused 11,000 minors between 1950 and 2002.

In the midst of this crisis, some lay people, fearing they had no rights or that their rights were woefully ignored, turned to civil authorities to prosecute allegations of sexual misconduct against clerics. Some believed that no recourse was available to them when the Church seemed to turn a deaf ear to their complaints. Commentators both within and outside the Church have expressed alarm or shock by the manner in which allegations have been received and often not prosecuted.

Many accused clerics, feeling powerless when they were removed from ministry or even the priesthood after allegations had been made, wondered about their own rights in the Church—especially the right of self-defense. Some maintain that they have been exposed to "double jeopardy" and "retried" for the same crime after they had been previously sanctioned. Others have maintained that they were never afforded due process in which to prove their innocence.

Participants of the Second Vatican Council (1962–1965) thought it opportune to present a series of rights based on the Council's formal teaching. These rights, understood as the protection to be afforded certain types of action on the basis of common humanity, had been articulated in earlier papal teaching. Popes like Leo XIII with *Rerum Novarum* and John XXIII with *Pacem in Terris* did much to promote the dignity of the human person and advocate for human rights in all spheres of society. Some years later, in 1983, some of these rights were to be formally adopted and legislated with the publication of a new *Code of Canon Law*. In addition to the "canonization" of some human rights in its legislation, the new Code also revised and updated its penal procedures, a development that has relevance to the recent sexual abuse investigations by Church authorities.

This book distills in a practical format the rights of Catholics now recognized in the Roman Catholic Church. Its purpose is really twofold: to familiarize Catholics with the rights and obligations written into Church law for all its members and to outline and demystify the procedures that are in place for the vindication of these rights. It is aimed at the interested Catholic in the pew, the lay ecclesial minister, and members of the clergy who have much at stake in the eventual resolution of the abuse crisis, but it has broader application as well. Many Catholics will be surprised to learn of their rights, not only as they relate to this crisis, but also in a variety of contexts and situations, including the right to choose a state of life and an appropriate "spirituality." Clergy will perhaps be surprised to see the small number of rights that are legislated in the Code particularly for them. But they may well be heartened to see the procedural protections that offer due process when allegations have been made against them. These are especially apparent in the new norms prepared by the United States Conference of

Catholic Bishops and approved by the Holy See for the prosecution of the crime of sexual abuse by a cleric. This book also elucidates various means at the disposal of all the Christian faithful in vindicating their rights.

The first part of the book will examine the various rights and obligations that are enumerated in the 1983 *Code of Canon Law*, under three categories: "the Christian faithful," "the laity," and "the clergy." *Christian faithful* is the term used to describe **all** those incorporated into Christ through baptism in the Church. Thus, all the rights that are identified in this section of the code would apply to all members of the Church, be they lay or cleric. The *laity*, as distinct from the *clergy*, make up most of the Church and are commissioned by virtue of their baptism to proclaim the gospel in their various walks of life. The ordained ministers are deacons, priests, and bishops who have been designated as such by the laying on of hands and prayer, for ministerial service to the community of the Church. Following the teachings of the Second Vatican Council, all members of the Christian faithful are equal in dignity and are called to work actively together for the building up of the Body of Christ.

Following each right listed in this first section is a description of the right, usually taken from the appropriate constitution or decree of the Second Vatican Council from which the right is derived. As will be seen, the Council documents provided the basis for much of the 1983 *Code of Canon Law*. In other words, the code legislated or defined as law the insights and teachings of the Council on the dignity of the human person and the fundamental rights of all. Both Pope Paul VI and Pope John Paul II carried this vision forward.

In each of these sections, the *obligations* of each group—Christian faithful, laity, and clergy—are also listed. Each baptized member of the Church is called to live in *communio*, "in communion," within the Church and with fellow members. Initiation into this community not only imparts rights but also various obligations that help protect and preserve the rights that are afforded to all for the sake of the common good.

When Pope John Paul II promulgated a new *Code of Canon Law* for the Church in 1983, it was promulgated for the Latin Rite. However, the Roman Catholic Church consists of twenty-two distinct churches: the Latin church and twenty-one Eastern Catholic churches, each with its own hierarchy, in communion with Rome. The canons of the Latin code affect members of the Latin church. In 1990, Pope John Paul II issued the *Code of Canons of the Eastern Churches* that affects members of the Eastern churches, unless otherwise specified. References in this text to canons about rights and obligations include both the Latin (CIC) and Eastern (CCEO) codes. The rights and obligations in both are almost identical.

Chapter 5 presents several flash points or hot spots in the church of today where questions about rights are being discussed. Examples, including admittance to the sacraments, the closing of parishes, and the allegation of sexual abuse against a cleric, attempt to address which rights come into play. Many times there are several rights and points of law that must be carefully considered.

One purpose for knowing rights is to give members of the Church a real possibility of vindicating those rights. There is a clear preference by the Church for due process in resolving issues of rights. The Church encourages use of a mediator or an arbitrator to resolve matters before utilizing other means of redress, although other means are provided. Included in chapter 6 is a sample process for resolving rights using a "due process" model presently used in the Archdiocese of Milwaukee (Wisconsin). It is important to note that bishops are empowered to establish and organize such processes for their own dioceses for the proper protection of rights and assurances of just proceedings in their jurisdiction.

The code also outlines a process for vindication of rights when attempts at due process, for one reason or another, fail or are inconclusive. A procedure called *hierarchical recourse* is outlined in Chapter 6. This is initiated when a member of the Christian faithful believes that he or she has been injured because of a decision given by a Church authority. Recourse is normally lodged against a bishop and involves an effort to remedy the situation locally before appealing to the appropriate Roman office. This appeal must be made within strictly prescribed time limits.

The appendices for this book include a full listing of the rights of the Christian faithful, the laity, and clerics as enumerated in the 1983 *Code of Canon Law*; a diagram containing the timeline and process for administrative recourse; and an outline of the procedures of the penal trial. This last process is used in cases such as the permanent removal of a priest from the clerical state.

This work is not, in any sense, a "do-it-yourself" guide to prosecuting individual rights when a member of the Church believes that his or her canonical rights have been violated. After attempts to resolve a dispute locally fail, a member of the Christian faithful may wish to consider a canonical process of recourse. In these cases it is important to secure the assistance of a qualified canon lawyer who is conversant with the norms of the procedures. A person would hire an attorney to help in civil proceedings; it only makes sense to take advantage of the expertise of canon lawyers when attempting formal recourse in Church matters. Normally, the names of competent canonists can be obtained from the local tribunal. Those filing complaints are advised in most cases to obtain an advocate (canon lawyer) from outside their own jurisdiction to ensure non-partiality.

It is hoped that as more members of the Christian faithful come to know their rights and more uniform efforts are made to observe and vindicate these rights, a more just Church will emerge. Only then can we be an appropriate reflection for society of what the Church teaches and preaches concerning the dignity of each human person.

I am most grateful for the guidance of several colleagues who reviewed the text and made many helpful suggestions and corrections: Rev. Thomas T. Brundage, Msgr. Frederick C. Easton, Rev. Patrick R. Lagges, Msgr. Roch Page, Dr. Michael Ritty, and Miss Linda Weigel. I wish to express gratitude for their expertise and the donation of precious time from their extremely busy canonical schedules.

AA   Decree on the Apostolate of the Laity, *Apostolicam Actuositatem*

AG   Decree on the Church's Missionary Activity, *Ad Gentes*

CCEO Code of Canons of the Eastern Churches, *Codex Canonum Ecclesiarum Orientalium*

CD   Decree on the Bishops' Pastoral Office in the Church, *Christus Dominus*

CIC   Code of Canon Law, *Codex Iuris Canonici*

DH   Declaration on Religious Freedom, *Dignitatis Humanae*

DV   Dogmatic Constitution on Divine Revelation, *Dei Verbum*

GE   Declaration on Christian Education, *Gravissimum Educationis*

GS   Pastoral Constitution on the Church in the Modern World, *Gaudium et Spes*

IM   Decree on the Instruments of Social Communication, *Inter Mirifica*

LG   Dogmatic Constitution on the Church, *Lumen Gentium*

NA   Declaration on the Relationship of the Church to Non-Christian Religions, *Nostra Aetate*

OE   Decree on Eastern Catholic Churches, *Orientalium Ecclesiarum*

OT   Decree on Priestly Formation, *Optatam Totius*

PB	Apostolic Constitution on the Roman Curia, *Pastor Bonus*
PC	Decree on the Appropriate Renewal of the Religious Life, *Perfectae Caritatis*
PJ	Promoter of Justice
PO	Decree on the Ministry and Life of Priests, *Presbyterorum Ordinis*
SC	Dogmatic Constitution on the Sacred Liturgy, *Sacrosanctum Concilium*
UR	Decree on Ecumenism, *Unitatis Reintegratio*

CHAPTER 1

The Development of Human Rights in the Church

The Roman Catholic Church has attempted, in view of its particular theological perspective of the human person, to provide a distinctive shape and context to the idea of human rights. Its Christian anthropological view of the human person helps differentiate a Catholic approach to rights from others that have their source in other religious and intellectual traditions.

The dignity of the human person has been the basis for the Catholic Church's teaching concerning human rights, especially as has been articulated in papal teaching during the last century. This teaching is grounded in the biblical account of the human person's creation in the image of God (Gn 1:28). The nature of this image has been interpreted in various ways in the Church's tradition. What appears fundamental are two central doctrines of Christianity: the Incarnation and the Redemption, by which the Christian tradition expresses its belief in the reality that God so loved the world that he became human. A specifically Christian warrant seeks to ground human rights in the dignity of the person, made in God's image and likeness.

The continuing attempt by the Church to express and clearly specify the claims of human dignity in every age has given rise to the development of the Roman Catholic human rights tradition. The last one hundred years have seen the promulgation of many papal encyclicals that attempt to articulate the centrality of human dignity and protection of the rights that flow from such concern. The teaching of the various popes about human rights has had an inevitable impact upon the Church's legal system or canon law. The legal apparatus seeks to recognize, guarantee, and foster the fundamental rights of the People of God as set forth in the Church's teaching on human rights.

Building on such encyclicals as *Rerum Novarum* (Leo XIII), which in 1891 addressed the rights of workers, Pope John XXIII promulgated the document *Pacem in Terris* in 1963. That encyclical effectively developed a human rights doctrine for the Catholic Church. It defends the dignity of the human person, reiterating and expanding the thought of previous encyclicals about social justice. Much of the argumentation of the document relies on reason and natural law, since it addresses rights that are the heritage of all people, and because this encyclical was addressed to "all people of good will." It affirms a wide variety of rights, including the right to life; the rights to clothing, food, and shelter; rest and medical care, culture, and education. It also addresses the right to freedom of expression, association, and the free exercise of religion. It speaks of the right to work, to organize, and to form labor unions. The rights to private property and to the juridical protection of one's rights are also mentioned.

The rights and obligations presented by John XXIII in *Pacem in Terris* are not unique in themselves, nor constitutive of a major departure from traditional Catholic thought. However, an effort was made in that encyclical to gather and list the rights in an explicit manner. The listing provided a basis for a critique of societies and their implementation of human rights. John XXIII saw the mutual acknowledgment of rights and obligations in a society as a kind of *preparatio evangelica*—a preparation for the gospel. It can bring the wider world to an awareness of fundamental values such as truth, justice, charity, and freedom that in turn can lead to knowledge of the true God—both personal and transcendent. *Pacem in Terris* demonstrated the concern of the Catholic human rights tradition to set specific rights within a moral context. To every human right there corresponds a duty that this right be respected by the subject of the right, by other individuals, and by the greater society. The protection and coordination of human rights is a responsibility that requires organized action by the entire society.

John XXIII's positioning of human rights within a natural law framework provided linkage with a central Catholic theological tradition. It also provided a parallel with the Western tradition that saw human rights as a development of positive law by moving the discussion to a "higher law" that affirmed natural and God-given rights. The freedom, dignity, rights, and responsibilities of each human person are sacred. The dignity of the person derives from his or her universal, inviolable, and inalienable rights. The human person has these rights because God the Creator has endowed each individual with intelligence and free will.

Pope John's theory of human rights contributed a natural law foundation to the discussion within the Roman Catholic tradition. This gave the Church the opportunity to dialogue with other cultures and states in an area of mutual concern. For the first time within its tradition, the Church provided an extended enumeration of human rights within a papal encyclical.

The Second Vatican Council underscored the Church's concern for human rights as developed in such encyclicals as

Pacem in Terris. For example, *Gaudium et Spes* ("The Church in the Modern World"), begins with a discussion of the human person's transcendental value, "[the human person] considered whole and entire, with body and soul, heart and conscience, mind and will" (GS, 3). Such an approach and anthropology lead to a Christian humanism focused on protecting individual rights and duties.

One of the major influences toward the incorporation of rights and their protection in the *Code of Canon Law* was the development of the *Principles for Revision* approved after the Council but before promulgation of the code. The 1967 Synod of Bishops approved these principles to provide a guide for the ongoing process of revising the code.

In April 1967, a central commission of consultors for the revision of the code, under the direction of Cardinal Pericle Felici, president of the commission, set out to develop several fundamental principles to aid in the task of revision. The resulting principles were reviewed and approved by the 1967 Synod. An important principle that emerged was the assurance of consistency between the revised law and the teachings of the Second Vatican Council. The principles thus tried to ensure that the new code emphasized the fundamental equality of all the faithful, and that appropriate judicial and administrative measures were created to protect the rights of persons against arbitrary uses of authority. The principles also affirmed that one of the essential objects of canon law is the determination and safeguarding of the rights and obligations of each person. One of the principles established that the revised code should acknowledge, define, and articulate the rights that the Christian faithful possess by law. Also mentioned was the need for implementing structures that would safeguard these rights.

In order to remove the dangers of arbitrariness in the exercise of authority, the principles called for a revised system of appeal for decisions and actions considered to be in violation of rights. They further state that in the pursuit of justice it would be necessary that such procedures be as open as possible and that the individual's rights be clearly identified and protected. The person against whom any accusations are made must be informed of all the charges made against him or her.

Toward the close of the Second Vatican Council, Pope Paul VI had suggested to the commission working on the revision of the code that they consider some type of "fundamental law of the Church." This *"Lex Ecclesiae Fundamentalis"* (LEF) would contain the essential theological and juridical bases of the Church and would be a kind of "constitution" upon which the rest of the new code could be structured. A sub-committee was assigned to this task and began working on a draft that among other things included a list of rights and duties that pertain to all the Christian faithful. Many of the rights were taken directly from the Council documents. An editorial decision was later made that eliminated rights and obligations as a separate part of the code. Instead, the rights and obligations would be incorporated within the respective sections of the Christian faithful, laity, and clergy.

The rights now included in the *Code of Canon Law* had their basis in a "constitutional statement," the *Lex Ecclesiae Fundamentalis*, and were uniquely mandated by "Principles for the Revision of the Code" of the 1967 Synod of Bishops. It is clear that these rights have a certain priority in the revised law of the Roman Catholic Church.

CHAPTER 2

The Christian Faithful

All the baptized constitute the "Christian faithful." Baptism has any number of effects, including sharing in the priestly, prophetic, and royal functions of Christ and exercising the mission that God has entrusted to the Church. Among the baptized, there are clerics and laity. The canons in this section of the code therefore address rights and obligations that would pertain to both the ordained and laypersons; however, some provisions may seem more pertinent to one vocation than to another. The canons reinforce that there exists among all the Christian faithful a true equality in which all contribute to the building up of the Body of Christ, according to each one's condition and function. The communion of all the Christian faithful amongst themselves and with the Church helps guide the implementation of rights and obligations, each person called to respect the dignity of the other and to work together in building up God's kingdom cooperatively.

Rights of the Christian Faithful

1. **Christ's faithful are free to make known their needs (CIC 212 §2, CCEO 15, §2).**

The Christian faithful are free to acknowledge their needs to those in the Church whom they believe can properly respond. Since this applies to rights derived from baptism (as do all the rights considered here), the needs most especially apply to spiritual concerns. Often times, as the Christian faithful have become more involved in the life of the Church (e.g., parish councils and diocesan synods), this activity can promote a better understanding of how various decisions affect their lives as well as their participation in the life of the diocese or parish. This right states that all the Christian faithful are free to raise questions and seek solutions to practical issues that are encountered in the life of a typical parish.

The Second Vatican Council asked the clergy to respect the dignity of the laity and to respect their just freedom. Toward that end, pastors should carefully listen to the wishes of the laity and recognize their experience and competence (PO 9). In fact, pastors are encouraged to enlist active participation by the laity in the life of the local church and parish, since their input can add to the wisdom of decisions that are made and strategies that are formulated that may impact the life of the local community. When the Christian faithful express their needs to their pastors, opportunity is given for creative reflection by both pastors and laity to engage in constructive dialogue for a shared collaboration in working toward acceptable solutions.

2. **The Christian faithful have the right to make known their opinions to pastors and other members of the Christian faithful (CIC 212 §3, CCEO 15, §3).**

One of the significant theological developments of the Second Vatican Council was its emphasis on *communio*, the understanding that the Church exists as a unity of local churches united in faith with a structured hierarchy. Although there is a variety of roles and offices in the Church, each individual participates according to his or her state in life. Although by virtue of this canon, each member of the Christian faithful has the right to express his or her opinions to pastors, certain extrinsic factors may influence the impact of their thoughts. Pastors will give key consideration to the knowledge and competence of those offering their opinions, as well as the theological quality and experience that form the opinion. What is clear and consistent from the Council documents is that pastors are called to listen carefully and with openness to the opinions that are sincerely and legitimately expressed. Not only did the Council recognize and encourage use of this right of expression of opinion, it insisted that it be done for the good of the Church (LG 37), if all the Christian faithful are to be "fellow-workers for the truth" (3 Jn 8). The right to express opinions should always be exercised with prudence and in charity.

3. **The Christian faithful have the right to receive assistance from their pastors (CIC 213, CCEO 16).**

The most important assistance that can be provided by the Church to its members comes from its spiritual resources. The Church is called to provide such assistance most especially through the Word of God and the sacraments. This right to spiritual nourishment and growth is one practical response of the more generic prior right, previously mentioned, i.e., the right of the Christian faithful to "make known their needs." Concurrent with this right is the obligation of pastors to make sure that all the Christian faithful are prepared to receive the sacraments.

> Pastors of souls and other members of the Christian faithful, according to their respective ecclesiastical functions, have the duty to take care that those who seek the sacraments are prepared to receive them by proper evangelization and catechetical instruction, attentive to the norms issued by competent authority. (CIC 843)

Increasingly problematic for the Church is its inability to provide in some areas, including the United States, its most important spiritual gift—the Eucharist—due to the decline in the number of ordained ministers.

4. **The Christian faithful have the right to worship God according to the prescriptions of their own rite (CIC 214, CCEO 17).**

There are twenty-two different rites in the Catholic Church, variously affected and formed by history, tradition, and culture. The Second Vatican Council made it clear that all such rites are to be respected and their respective spiritualities and liturgical expressions to be encouraged. It is the hope of the Church that each individual rite retain its tradition, whole and entire, "while adjusting its way of life to the various needs of time and place" (OE 2). The Council attempted to encourage the proper respect for each of the rites by insisting that baptized members of non-Catholic churches desiring to enter into full communion with the Catholic Church do so by retaining his or her proper rite. In other words, the baptized person enters the Catholic Church through the rite most similar to his or her original one.

5. **The Christian faithful have the right to found and govern their own associations (CIC 215, CCEO 18).**

A basic natural right recognized by the Church is for members to gather together, using their resources to work effectively for apostolic endeavors: charity, social justice, etc. The types of associations that are formed have various levels of official recognition by the Church. Such joint efforts show concretely the call by the Council to promote efforts by all members of the Church to participate in its mission. By pooling their resources to achieve the aims of the apostolate, it is often more likely that the ends of the work can be more easily accomplished. The right to form labor unions is among the basic rights of association identified by recent popes. "These unions should be truly able to represent the workers and contribute to the proper arrangement of economic life. Another such right is that of taking part freely in the activity of those unions without risk of reprisal" (GS 68).

6. The Christian faithful have the right to promote and to sustain apostolic action (CIC 216; CCEO 19).

By virtue of their baptism, all the Christian faithful have the right and duty to promote the gospel, as disciples of the Lord Jesus. This right is, however, exercised according to the particular state in life of the Christian and under the supervision of the hierarchy. The Second Vatican Council strongly encouraged the hierarchy to recognize this right.

> "Bishops, pastors and other priests of both branches of the clergy should keep in mind that the right and duty to exercise the apostolate is common to all the faithful, both clergy and laity, and that the laity also have their own proper roles in building up the Church." (AA 25)

7. The Christian faithful have a right to a Christian education (CIC 217; CCEO 20).

This right to an education is a human right by virtue of the dignity of each person. The Church insists on Christian education for all its faithful so that its members come to know and appreciate the faith. The Christian transformation of the world is premised closely on the assumption that the Christian has been educated in the truth and therefore helps contribute to the good of society as a whole.

> Since every Christian has become a new creature by rebirth from water and the Holy Spirit, so that [the Christian] may be called what he [or she] truly is, a child of God, [the Christian] is entitled to a Christian education. (GE 2)

Parents have a special obligation, as will be seen in the "rights of the laity," to make sure that a Christian education is provided for their children. With the emphasis given by the Council to the participation of all members of the Christian faithful in the apostolic mission of the Church, it is crucial that they receive an appropriate education about their faith. Christian education will also be essential in many cases for certain positions or offices that are now available to be exercised by laity.

8. The Christian faithful possess a lawful freedom of inquiry (CIC 218; CCEO 21).

Those who engage in the "sacred sciences" are to have a freedom of inquiry as they approach their specific disciplines. Such fields of study encompass areas that seek to understand and appreciate the faith. Theologians enjoy a rightful opportunity for inquiry in their discipline, while observing a proper respect for and submission to the magisterium. By encouraging and respecting the freedom of inquiry, the Church promotes dialogue between the secular and religious spheres.

> [The Church] intends thereby to promote an ever deeper understanding of these fields, and as a result of extremely precise evaluation of modern problems and inquiries, to have it seen more profoundly how faith and reason give harmonious witness to the unity of all truth. (GE 10)

9. The Christian faithful have the right to choose a state of life (CIC 219; CCEO 22).

No member of the Christian faithful can be forced or coerced into making a vocational choice. The Church can help to promote means by which its members are helped in discerning this important decision. But there is no guarantee of, nor any implication of the right to a specific vocation. It is, for example, the role of the bishop with the assistance of the local community to discern the possible presence of a vocation to ministerial service. This right—a basic human right—flows from the dignity of the human person.

> [T]here is growing awareness of the exalted dignity proper to the human person, since [the individual] stands above all things, and his [and her] rights and duties are universal and inviolable. (GS 26)

10. The members of the Christian faithful have the right to a good reputation and the protection of their privacy (CIC 220; CCEO 23).

No one is permitted to harm illegitimately the good reputation that a person enjoys, nor may anyone violate the right of any person to protect his or her privacy. One of the most valuable possessions of each person is his or her reputation. The right to this reputation is a human right that derives from the dignity of the person. This right and the protection of reputation have achieved recent attention in the prosecution of clerics for possible sexual misconduct crimes. It is important that investigations in this matter proceed prudently and carefully, and that no one's good name—accuser or accused—be damaged irresponsibly.

The Church has also defended the right of the Christian faithful to privacy, especially psychological privacy, with various protections concerning unauthorized self-disclosure, e.g., by insisting that such evaluations be agreed to by the accused in any penal process.

11. The Christian faithful have the right to vindicate and defend their rights (CIC 221 §1; CCEO 24 §1).

The Christian faithful can vindicate and defend the rights they possess in the Church in an ecclesiastical forum, according to the norm of law. It is not sufficient to enumerate and promote rights if there are not mechanisms, procedures, and forums where rights may be vindicated when challenged.

This canon states the acknowledgement by Church law of the very basic human right of defense when a right or rights are challenged or ignored, based on the dignity of the human person. For example, no penalties may be imposed upon the Christian faithful unless in accordance with the norm of law. Preceding any litigation, parties are encouraged to utilize due process.

One of the challenges now facing the Church is to design effective court procedures for dealing with disputes. For the most part, the only tribunals available are marriage tribunal courts that are usually overwhelmed with a large number of marriage nullity cases. Some dioceses are experimenting with administrative tribunals (see chapter 6) that would use a combination of due process and the court procedures outlined in the *Code of Canon Law*.

If a controversy is the result of an administrative act (usually an official decision by a person in authority, given in writing) the avenue of challenge to the decision must be made through the superior using the procedure called "hierarchic recourse" outlined in CIC 1732–1739, CCEO 996–1006 (see chapter 6). This procedure involves petitioning the superior to rescind or modify the original decision within prescribed time limits. If the appellant is not satisfied with the response of the superior to the appeal, recourse can then be made to that person's "hierarchic superior" to overturn the decision, again, within prescribed time limits.

12. The law is to be applied equitably (CIC 221 §2; CCEO 24, §2)

If a member of the Christian faithful is summoned to a trial by a competent authority, that member has the right to be judged according to the prescriptions of the law and to justice applied with mercy (equity). The equality of all the

Christian faithful must be acknowledged in the Church's legal procedures. Any person who is summoned to a trial proceeding after being charged with the commission of a canonical offense has the right to the process and procedures outlined in the code of canon law, administered fairly and justly. The person has the right to an advocate (CIC 1738, CCEO 1003), as well as to his or her reputation and good name while the charges are examined.

13. The Christian faithful may not be punished except in accordance with the norm of law (CIC 221, §2, CCEO 24, §3).

Members of the Church may not be punished with canonical penalties except by the norm of law. In order to make sure that the rights of all parties are protected in a canonical process that could possibly impose a penalty, it is important that the norms of law be applied carefully. The one alleged must be a violation of law that is established in the law itself. The elements of due process must be provided, including the right of defense, canonical counsel, ability to review the acts of the case that have been assembled, and the right to make an appeal against the sentence or a recourse against an administrative decision. That penalties should be imposed only as a last resort is also a canonical principle recognized in law.

Obligations of the Christian Faithful

1. Christian faithful are to cooperate in building up the Body of Christ (CIC 208; CCEO 11).

Due to their rebirth in Christ through baptism, there exists among all the Christian faithful a true equality regarding dignity and action by which they all cooperate in the building up of the Body of Christ according to each person's condition and function. By virtue of their baptism, the Christian faithful become members of the People of God and enter into relationship with the other baptized. "This very diversity of graces, ministries, and works gathers the children of God into one, because 'all these are the work of one and the same Spirit'" (LG 32).

2. **The Christian faithful are called to maintain communion with the Church (c. 209, §1; CCEO 12).**

The Christian faithful, even in their manner of acting, are always obliged to maintain communion with the Church. Just as all the members of the Christian faithful are called to use their talents and gifts to participate in the Church's mission, they are likewise called to maintain unity with the Body of Christ. "The faithful in their turn should enthusiastically lend their cooperative assistance to their pastors and teachers. Thus in their diversity all bear witness to the admirable unity of the Body of Christ" (LG 32).

3. **Christian faithful are called to lead a holy life and to promote the growth of the Church (CIC 210; CCEO 13).**

All the Christian faithful must direct their efforts to lead a holy life and to promote the growth of the Church and its continual sanctification, according to their own condition. One of the opportunities given to each member of the Christian faithful in spreading the gospel is by living a lifestyle that demonstrates a commitment to the values of Jesus Christ.

> The very testimony of their Christian life, and good work done in the supernatural spirit, have the power to draw [people] to belief and to God; for the Lord says, "Even so let your light shine before men, in order that they may see your

good works and give glory to your Father in heaven"(Mt 5:16). (AA 6)

4. The Christian faithful have an obligation to promote the message of salvation (CIC 211: CCEO 14).

All the Christian faithful have the duty and right to work so that the divine message of salvation reaches all people. The Church has received a mandate from Christ to proclaim the message of salvation to the ends of the earth. The Church sees itself as "missionary" by nature, called at every time and in every place to preach the gospel.

> The pilgrim Church is missionary by her very nature. For it is from the mission of the Son and the mission of the Holy Spirit that she takes her origin, in accordance with the decree of God the Father. (AG 2)

All members are called to participate in this effort:

> Therefore, all sons [and daughters] of the Church should have a lively awareness of their responsibility to the world. They should foster in themselves a truly Catholic spirit. They should spend their energies in the work of evangelization. (AG 36)

It was the hope of the Council that the newly energized Christian faithful would help cause new spiritual inspiration to sweep over the whole Church (AG 36).

5. The Christian faithful are called to follow their pastors (CIC 212 §1: CCEO 15).

Conscious of their own responsibility, the Christian faithful are called to follow those things that the pastors declare as teachers of the faith. It is the belief of the Church that Christ has entrusted responsibility to the bishops for teaching the truths of the Christian faith. "In matters of faith and morals, the bishops speak in the name of Christ and the faithful are to accept their teaching and adhere to it with a religious assent of the soul" (LG 25). At the same time, the Second Vatican Council has insisted that its leaders give proper respect to the opinions and needs of all the Christian faithful.

> Priests should also confidently entrust to the laity duties in the service of the Church, allowing them freedom and room for action. In fact, on suitable occasions, they should invite them to undertake works on their own initiative. (PO 9)

6. The Christian faithful are called to assist with the needs of the Church (CIC 222 §1; CCEO 25 §1).

The Church, in its efforts to proclaim the gospel message, is always in need of material support by all its members. The Christian faithful are called in virtue of their baptism to participate in the Church's mission and assist not only by action on its behalf, but by material support as well. Such support takes various forms: free will offerings, remuneration for those who exercise ordained ministry and other Christian faithful who devote themselves to ministry, and financial resources to underwrite various apostolates or to fund temporal goods needed to sustain efforts that promote the gospel.

7. The Christian faithful have the obligation to promote social justice (CIC 222 §2: CCEO 25 §2).

The Christian faithful are called to promote the gospel in their daily lives. The Church, especially since the encyclicals of Pope Leo XIII, has attempted to forcefully apply the gospel to modern social issues such as labor issues of the industrial age. The Christian faithful are called to study the encyclicals and other teachings of the Church in the area of social justice. Thus, they may take practical steps to apply the teachings of the gospel to concrete modern realities. At the heart of such teachings is the dignity of the human person that spurs on the Christian faithful to efforts in daily life to ensure that this dignity is preserved and appropriately defended.

8. **The Christian faithful are to consider the common good when exercising their rights (c. 223 §1; CCEO 26, §1).**

Although the rights of the Christian faithful are directed toward an affirmation of the dignity of the individual, there is a need to take into consideration the good of the community when the rights are exercised. The Second Vatican Council recognized this good when it addressed the individual and the larger community where the person functions, "the sum total of the conditions of social life enabling groups and individuals to realize their perfection more fully and readily" (GS 26). Such an emphasis in the exercise of rights reinforces the association of the exercise of rights and the larger mission of the Church.

CHAPTER 3

The Laity

In addition to the rights and obligations of the Christian faithful, the canons also explicitly address the rights and obligations of the laity. The laity are those members of the Christian faithful whose ministry derives solely from their baptism. They have not received ordination but work within the world for the proclamation of the Gospel. The laity live out their baptismal promises in their everyday lives in a variety of professions and circumstances. Each lay person must answer to the Lord's call to holiness, both as individuals and in cooperation with others to build up the kingdom of God here on Earth. It happens frequently that only through the efforts of lay Catholics will some people come to know Christ and the gospel.

One of the key emphases in this section will be the role of the family and the obligation of the laity to work through marriage in building up the people of God. Parents have a most serious responsibility to educate their children in the ways of the faith. The whole Church is likewise enjoined to assist parents in this important effort.

Rights of the Laity

1. **Married Christians have the right to imbue the world with their charisms and spirituality (CIC 226 §1: CCEO 400).**

The Second Vatican Council emphasized the equality of all the faithful. The rights of the laity as listed in this section of the code clearly demonstrate the crucial role of the laity in the mission of the Church when they use their specific charisms to actively engage in the apostolate.

> The lay apostolate [. . .] is a participation in the saving mission of the Church itself. Through their baptism and confirmation, all are commissioned to that apostolate by the Lord Himself. (LG 33)

The laity are called to live out their baptismal promises in their daily lives.

> Now the laity are called in a special way to make the Church present and operative in those places and circumstances where only through them can she become the salt of the earth. (LG 33)

The laity influence their environment by living gospel values each day.

> Their main duty, whether they are men or women, is the witness which they are bound to bear to Christ by their life and work in the home, in the social group, and in their own professional circle. (AG 21)

2. **The lay Christian faithful have the right to educate their children (CIC 226 §2, CCEO 627 §1, CCEO 627 §3).**

Since they have given life to their children, parents (and by extension those who take their place) have the obligation and right to educate them. "Their role as educators is so decisive that scarcely anything can compensate for their failure in it" (GE 3). Parents are to educate their children in the context of a Christian family, illumined by faith. They share this important responsibility with the assistance of pastors who are likewise concerned with education of children and their growth in the faith. Parents have the right to choose the best means by which their children will be endowed with strong Christian values. Society has a great stake in this education as well, since "the family is the first school of those social virtues which every society needs" (GE 3).

3. **The lay Christian faithful have the right to freedom as citizens (CIC 227; CCEO 402).**

Lay Christian faithful have the right to freedom in secular affairs that belong to all citizens. Their participation flows from their human right to involvement in the affairs of state, based on the inherent dignity of the individual. Their actions and activities, however, should be imbued with the spirit of the gospel. The Church has its own responsibility to inform the society in which it lives with moral teachings.

> As regards activities and institutions in the temporal order, the role of the ecclesiastical hierarchy is to teach and authentically interpret the moral principles to be followed in temporal affairs. (AA 24)

4. **The lay Christian faithful have the right to assume ecclesiastical offices when qualified (CIC 228 §1, CCEO 408 §2).**

Laypersons who are suitable are qualified to be admitted by pastors to ecclesiastical offices that they are able to exercise according to the norms of law. Since the Second Vatican Council and the 1983 *Code of Canon Law*, the laity have exercised offices in the Church, including chancellor, finance officer, etc. Their appointment is dependent upon the competence of the individual to fulfill the qualifications of the particular office. Such efforts are an attempt to make practicable the call by the Council to recognize the baptismal responsibilities and gifts of the laity.

> Finally, the Fathers of the Council believe it would be most advantageous if these same departments would give a greater hearing to lay [persons] who are outstanding for their virtue, knowledge, and experience. Thus they, too, will have an appropriate share in Church affairs. (CD 10)

5. **The lay Christian faithful have the right to act as advisors to pastors (CIC 228 §2; CCEO 408 §2).**

With the necessary knowledge, prudence, and integrity, lay persons assist pastors of the Church as experts and advisors, either as individual consultors or as members of councils or various assemblies, whether parochial or diocesan. The Church has been greatly enhanced by the participation of the laity in its organizational life. Considerable skill and talent have been shared by the laity by virtue of their secular employment, particularly administrative and financial skills. It is important that pastors recognize and promote these gifts.

> Let sacred pastors recognize and promote the dignity as well as the responsibility of the lay [person] in the Church. Let them willingly make use of his [and her] prudent advice. Let them confidently assign duties [. . .] in the service of the Church, allowing [. . .] freedom and room for action. Further, let them [the pastors] consider [. . .] the projects, suggestions and desires proposed by the laity. (LG 37)

It was to utilize these gifts that the Council wished to establish a diocesan pastoral council that would include laity, religious, and clergy to advise the diocesan bishop. Such councils, when erected, would "investigate and . . . weigh matters which bear on pastoral activity and . . . formulate practical conclusions regarding them" (CD 27).

6. **Lay Christian faithful have the right to acquire knowledge of Christian doctrine (CIC 229 §1; CCEO 404 §1). They also possess the right to acquire the fuller knowledge of the sacred sciences taught in ecclesiastical universities and to obtain appropriate degrees (CIC 229 §2; CCEO 404 §2). They also have the right, when properly qualified and with requisite suitability, to receive a mandate from ecclesiastical authority to teach the sacred sciences (CIC 229 §3; CCEO 404 §3).**

The laity have the right to acquire knowledge of Christian doctrine to lead them to a deeper understanding of their faith. Such study also helps them in their increasing participation in the life of the Church.

> The disciple is bound by a grave obligation toward Christ. . . ever more adequately to understand the truth received from Him, faithfully to proclaim it, and vigorously to defend it . . . . (DH 14)

> Let the laity strive skillfully to acquire a more profound grasp of revealed truth, and insistently beg of God the gift of wisdom. (LG 35)

Many laypersons are engaged in professional studies to equip them in their roles or employment as church ministers. Many have gone on to advanced studies—including university level—for degrees in scripture, theology, etc. Such an education not only benefits the Church, but also has the ability to affect the surrounding culture.

The hoped-for result is that the Christian mind may achieve, as it were, a public, persistent and universal presence in the whole enterprise of advancing higher culture, and that the students of these institutions may become truly outstanding in learning, ready to shoulder society's heavier burdens and to witness the faith to the world. (GE 10)

Competent and qualified laypersons may seek a mandate that permits them to teach in the name of the Church, from the appropriate ecclesiastical authority.

Worthy of special praise are those lay [people] who work in universities or in scientific institutions and whose historical and scientificreligious research promotes knowledge of peoples and of religions. (AG 41)

7. **Laypersons have the right to decent remuneration when employed by the Church (CIC 231 § 2; CCEO 409 §2).**

Lay persons have the right to appropriate remuneration so that they can provide decently for their own needs and those of their families. They also have the right to suitable insurance, social security, and health care. The Church's teaching on social justice in the workplace and the dignity of the worker must find a home in the wages and benefits of those who are employed in Church ministries. These benefits include those required by the civil jurisdiction for employees.

The pastors of the Church should gladly and gratefully welcome these lay persons and make sure that their situation meets the demands of justice, equity, and charity to the fullest extent possible, particularly as regards proper support for them and their families. (AA 22)

Obligations of the Laity

1. **The lay members of the Christian faithful are obliged to work individually or in groups to proclaim the divine message (CIC 225 §1; CCEO 401).**

As members of the baptized Christian faithful, the laity share in the Church's mission of proclaiming the gospel. They share in the priestly, prophetic, and royal office of Christ (AA 2) and have their role to play in the mission of the whole People of God in the Church and in the world.

> Now the laity are called in a special way to make the Church present and operative in those places and circumstances where only through them can she become the salt of the earth. (LG 33)

2. **The lay Christian faithful have the obligation to perfect the temporal order (CIC 225 §2; CCEO 406).**

The laity by their baptism carry out their own special mission within the Church to the world. "Everywhere and in all things they must seek the justice characteristic of God's kingdom" (AA 7). This involves them in their surrounding cultures, economic affairs, the arts, professions, and a variety of political institutions. Their special responsibility is to imbue the world in which they live, work, and play with the light of Jesus Christ, especially by their daily commitment to living his values and message.

> But the laity, by their very vocation, seek the kingdom of God by engaging in temporal affairs and by ordering them according to the plan of God. They live in the world, that is, in each and in all the secular professions and occupations.

They live in the ordinary circumstances of family and social life, from which the very web of their existence is woven. (LG 31)

The involvement of the laity in the daily affairs of the secular world should result in a Christian impact on those with whom they interact.

They [the laity] are called there by God so that by exercising their proper functions and being led by the spirit of the gospel they can work for the sanctification of the world from within, in the manner of leaven. In this way they can make Christ known to others, especially by the testimony of a life resplendent in faith, hope and charity. (LG 31)

3. **The lay Christian faithful build up the kingdom by their married vocation and family life (CIC 226 §1: CCEO 407).**

The Church recognizes and extols the family as the basic unit of society. The Council identified and recognized the key role of parents in the education of their children in the ways of faith, being the first to communicate gospel living to their children.

It has always been the duty of Christian couples, but today it is the supreme task of their apostolate, to manifest and prove by their own way of life the unbreakable and sacred character of the marriage bond, to affirm vigorously the right and duty of parents and guardians to educate children in a Christian manner, and to defend the dignity and lawful independence of the family. (AA 11)

Efforts that promote strong family life should be undertaken in order that these values be preserved in society.

> They [the laity] and the rest of the faithful, there-
> fore, should cooperate . . . to ensure the preserva-
> tion of these rights in civil legislation, and to
> make sure that attention is paid to the needs of
> the family in government policies, regarding
> housing, the education of children, working con-
> ditions, social security, and taxes. . . . (AA 11)

Such concern must also be extended to children who lack the blessings of a family. They need to be protected by prudent legislation and various undertakings on their behalf (GS 52).

CHAPTER 4

The Clergy

This section of the code deals with those who have received ordination to sacred ministry. Both priests and deacons are included in the term "cleric." However, some canons will specifically address priests or deacons regarding certain prescriptions of the law. Those offices in the Church that require the power of holy orders or the power of ecclesiastical governance are limited to clerics. Some offices (e.g., pastor) require that the office holder be a priest.

The Second Vatican Council encouraged an attitude of fraternity between bishops and their priests. The bishop is exhorted to know his priests individually and well, so that he may assist and encourage them in their ministry. At the same time, clerics are called to respect those who exercise the ministry of bishop in their midst, recognizing the difficulty of the role of overseer, and actively cooperating in the Lord's work with him. It is within a spirit of trust and mutual respect that the obligations and rights of clerics are to be understood and exercised.

Rights of the Clergy

1. Clerics have a right to appropriate remuneration (CIC 281 §1: CCEO 390 §1).

Since clerics dedicate themselves to ecclesiastical ministry, they deserve remuneration that is consistent with their condition, taking into account the nature of their function and the conditions of places and times. Such remuneration should assure that they are able to provide for the necessities of their lives as well as equitable payment for those whose service they need. Their remuneration should also permit them to take a vacation each year. If the cleric is married (Eastern Catholic Churches) remuneration must be adequate for the support of his family, unless this is otherwise sufficiently provided for (CCEO 390 §1).

The Second Vatican Council also called for clerics to embrace a simple lifestyle.

> Led, therefore by the Lord's Spirit, who anointed the Savior to preach the gospel to the poor, priests as well as bishops will avoid all those things that offend the poor in any way. (PO 17)

The rectories or houses in which they live should likewise give witness to gospel values:

> Let them have the kind of dwelling which will appear closed to no one and which no one will fear to visit, even the humblest. (PO 17)

2. Clerics should receive the appropriate social assistance and benefits (CIC 281 §2: CCEO 390 §2).

Provision should be made so that clerics may possess the social assistance that provides for their needs suitably if they suffer from illness, incapacity, or old age. Married clerics (Eastern Catholic Churches) should have the appropriate benefits available for their families. In order for this right to be put into practice effectively, clerics are obliged to contribute to a special fund mentioned in c. 1021 (CCEO) in accordance with particular law (CCEO 390 §2).

3. **Permanent deacons should receive provisions for their family (CIC 281 §3; CCEO 390 §2).**

Married deacons who devote themselves completely to ecclesiastical ministry deserve remuneration which enables them to provide for the support of themselves and their families. Those deacons who receive recompense by secular employment should make sure that their needs and those of their families are met.

4. **Clerics are to be provided a sufficient period for vacation (CIC 283 §2; CCEO 392).**

Clerics are entitled to a fitting and sufficient time of vacation each year as determined by universal or particular law. Universal law provides four weeks of vacation for a pastor, not including retreat time (CIC 533 §2). The month may be continuous or spread out over the year.

5. **Clerics have the right to obtain from their eparchial bishop, after the requirements of law have been satisfied, a certain office or ministry or function to be exercised in the service of the Church (CCEO 371 §1).**

Unlike in the Latin code, clerics of the Eastern Catholic Churches have the right to obtain from their eparch (equivalent to Latin Rite "bishop") an assignment to ministry, provided that all requirements of the law have been satisfied (e.g., proper incardination into a diocese). There is no equivalent canon in the Latin code that concedes to the cleric a right to an assignment.

Special Obligations of the Clergy

1. **Clerics have the obligation to show reverence and obedience to the Roman Pontiff and to their own Ordinary (CIC 273; CCEO 370).**

   In virtue of ordination, a special relationship is established between the cleric and his bishop that includes a sense of mutual respect and cooperation. A cleric owes obedience in those areas that are prescribed specifically in the law. As the cleric participates in the mission of the Church, organizational concerns make it imperative that clergy work cooperatively with their bishop.

   > All priests, together with bishops, so share in one and the same priesthood and ministry of Christ that the very unity of their consecration and mission requires their hierarchical communion with the order of bishops. (PO 7)

2. **Clerics are obliged to fulfill the duties of pastoral ministry that are entrusted to them (CIC 274, §2; CCEO 371 §2, CIC 276, §2, 1°; CCEO 368) and thus foster peace and harmony (CIC 287 §1; CCEO 384).**

   These canons address the practical implementation of the bond between the bishop and his clergy, such as in the matter of assignments to ministry. The Council documents make it clear that assignments come to the cleric from his bishop, although in many dioceses, bishops are assisted in these decisions by personnel boards, members of which are often elected by the clergy themselves. Since such arrangements are an effort to involve the clergy more fully in the assignment process, it would seem important that bishops review carefully the recommendations that come to them from such boards before making clergy assignments.

Clerics are ministers working to bring about peace and harmony by their proclamation of the gospel. Such ministry is to be devoid of any affiliation with an ideology.

> In building the Christian community, priests are never to put themselves at the service of any ideology or human faction. Rather as heralds of the gospel and shepherds of the Church, they must devote themselves to the spiritual growth of the Body of Christ. (PO 6)

3. **Clergy are to maintain a bond of brotherhood and prayer with other clerics (CIC 275 §1: CCEO 379).**

Although individually ordained to ministry, clergy are to be united in mission even though normally serving in an individual assignment.

> Established in the priestly order by ordination, all priests are united among themselves in an intimate sacramental brotherhood. In a special way they form one presbytery in a diocese to whose service they are committed under their bishop. For even though priests are assigned to different duties they still carry on one priestly ministry. . . . (PO 8)

Clerics are also to have compassion and concern for their brothers with whom they minister.

> Inspired by a fraternal spirit, priests will not neglect hospitality, but cultivate kindliness and share their goods in common. They will be particularly solicitous for priests who are sick, afflicted, overburdened with work, lonely, exiled form their homeland, or suffering persecution. (PO 8)

4. **Clerics are to promote the mission of the laity (CIC 275 §2; CCEO 381 §3).**

Clergy are called to recognize and promote the gifts possessed by the laity and assist them in their own mission and ministry.

> Bishops, pastors, and other priests . . . should keep in mind that the right and duty to exercise the apostolate is common to all the faithful, both clergy and laity, and that the laity also have their own proper roles in building up the Church. (AA 25)

> Clergy are to listen to the needs of all the faithful. Priests must sincerely acknowledge and promote the dignity of the laity and the role which is proper to them in the mission of the Church. . . . They should listen to the laity willingly, consider their wishes in a fraternal spirit, and recognize their experience and competence in the different areas of human activity, so that together with them they will be able to read the signs of the times. (PO 9)

5. **Clerics are to pursue holiness (CIC 276 §1; CCEO 368), by nourishing their spiritual life from word and table (CIC 276 §2, 2°; CCEO 369) and utilizing mental prayer (CIC 276 §2, 5°). Their spirituality includes recitation of the liturgy of the hours (CIC 276 §2, 3°) and making at least annual retreats (CIC 276 §2, 4°; CCEO 369 §2).**

Like all members of the Christian faithful, clerics are called, by virtue of their baptism, to conform themselves to the gospel and the life of Jesus Christ.

> In the various types and duties of life, one and the same holiness is cultivated by all who are moved by the Spirit of God and who obey the voice of the Father, worshipping God the Father

in spirit and in truth. These souls follow the poor Christ, the humble and cross bearing Christ, in order to be made worthy of being partakers in His glory. Every person should walk unhesitatingly according to his own personal gifts and duties in the path of a living faith that arouses hope and works through charity. (LG 41)

The Council documents provide clear guidance for the particular spirituality of the cleric:

Priests will attain sanctity in a manner proper to them if they exercise their offices sincerely and tirelessly in the Spirit of Christ. Since they are ministers of God's Word, they should every day read and listen to that Word which they are required to teach to others. If they are at the same time preoccupied with welcoming this message into their own hearts they will become ever more perfect disciples of the Lord. (PO 13)

One practical means of scripture meditation is the recitation of the liturgy of the hours, in which psalmody and scripture is prayed daily. The cleric is also obliged to spend some time each year on an extended retreat, away from his normal pastoral obligations in order that by quiet time in prayerful reflection he may ground himself more intensely in the ministry in which he is engaged.

6. **Clerics are called to perfect and perpetual continence and to exercise due prudence in this regard (CIC 277 §1; CCEO 373, CIC 277 §2; CCEO 374).**

The requirement of celibacy is not demanded by the nature of priesthood itself, as can be seen in the tradition of the Eastern Churches. Also, the permanent diaconate accepts candidates for service who are already married. However, the tradition of the Western Church has esteemed clerical celibacy as an appropriate way to follow Christ in ministry.

> With respect to the priestly life, the Church has always held in especially high regard perfect and perpetual continence on behalf of the kingdom of God. Such continence was recommended by Christ the Lord. (PO 16)

7. **Secular clerics have the right to associate with others for ends appropriate to their state in life (CIC 278 §1; CCEO 391).**

As has been previously acknowledged, all the Christian faithful have a natural right to enter into associations in order to achieve ends consistent and consonant with the apostolate (CIC 215, CCEO 18). Likewise, clerics by virtue of this canon have the right to form associations whose statutes have been approved by the competent authority and whose purpose is to foster holiness in the exercise of ministry (PO 8).

8. **Clerics are called to a simple style of life (CIC 282 §1; CCEO 385 §1), to live a life in community when possible (CIC 280, CCEO 376), and to wear suitable ecclesiastical garb (CIC 284; CCEO 387). They are to avoid those things that are unbecoming to their clerical state (CIC 285; CCEO 382;) and not to leave the diocese for extended periods (CIC 283 §1; CCEO 386 §1).**

Clerics are to live a life detached from possessions. They are to embrace a simplicity of lifestyle that reflects the example of Christ who conducted his ministry freed from many attachments and who identified himself with the poor.

> Led, therefore, by the Lord's Spirit, who anointed the Savior and sent Him to preach the gospel to the poor, priests as well as bishops will avoid all those things which can offend the poor in any way. (PO 17)

Clerics must be careful to avoid all those things that would be unbecoming to their state of life, especially that which has been regulated by particular law. Their dwellings should likewise have the appearance of simplicity. " . . . [L]et them have the kind of dwelling which will appear closed to no one and which no one will fear to visit, even the humblest" (PO 17).

Priests are encouraged to live a community life when possible. While this will vary greatly according to circumstances and ministry, it offers them the opportunity to give mutual support to their brothers and always "help one another to be fellow workers on behalf of truth" (PO 8). Clerics are to be publicly identifiable when exercising their ministry by wearing suitable ecclesiastical garb, which is determined by the appropriate conference of bishops after taking into account the local custom.

9. **Priests are not to run for elected office (CIC 285 §3; CCEO 383 1°), nor are they to be involved in political parties or trade unions (CIC 287 §2; CCEO 384 §2). They are not to engage in business or trade without permission (CIC 286; CCEO 385 §2), nor are they to be agents for goods belonging to lay persons (CIC 285 §4; CCEO 385 §2).**

The ministry of the priest is not to be compromised by a particular affiliation with a political party or with trade unions that may take stands that compromise Church teaching. Many times, a priest may more effectively critique and challenge the political system from a distance. As a member of a political party or as an elected official, he may be compromised when votes cast reflect a position at variance with the gospel or Church teachings.

Given the Council's call to an abstemious lifestyle that appropriately reflects Jesus, the itinerant preacher and carpenter's son, it is understandable that the law would caution against clerics serving as agents for goods belonging to lay persons or engaging in business or trade without the permission of their ordinary.

10. **Clerics are not to engage in military service without permission of their ordinary (CIC 289 §2; CCEO 283 2°) and should make use of proper exemptions for duties alien to the clerical state (CIC 289 §2, CCEO 283 3°).**

Clerics are often called in their ministry to speak to the gospel themes of peace and justice and to work toward a ministry of reconciliation. It may be inappropriate for them to serve in the military when it has the possibility of inflicting harm on the innocent. This does not preclude the possibility of clerics serving as chaplains in the armed forces. The Church likewise has encouraged clerics to seek exemptions from such activities as jury duty when the possibility exists that such juries may be called upon to offer punishments that are not in keeping with the Church's position on such matters, i.e., capital punishment.

CHAPTER 5

Some Specific Issues in the Church Today

Rights and the Sacraments

1. Can parents be denied the sacrament of baptism for their children?

Frequently one or both parents presenting their child for baptism are not practicing their faith. For whatever reason, the faith of the parent(s) may have grown dormant. Sometimes an encounter with a representative of the Church has resulted in a feeling of alienation on the part of the parents. Or perhaps the practice of religious faith has never been a vital part of *their* upbringing. This is a delicate challenge to the pastoral minister, conscious that the baptismal rites are addressed to cooperating and practicing members of the faith community.

Parents are obliged to see to it that infants are baptized within the first weeks after birth and are to be properly prepared for it (CIC 867 §1, CCEO 686 §). There must, however, be a well-founded hope that the infant will be brought up in the Catholic faith before the sacrament may be administered. If such hope is altogether lacking, the baptism is to be delayed and the parents informed of this decision (CIC 868, §2, CCEO 681 §1, §4).

Each diocese should have policies regarding the deferring of the sacrament. Pastoral experience over the years seems to indicate that outright refusal is a violation of the right to the sacraments and rarely results in a return to the Church. In fact, it may permanently estrange the parents from the practice of the faith. Most often, a patient and persistent approach in educating parents to the connection between the meaning of the sacrament, the faith of the child, and the parents' faith life can lead to the establishment of a well-founded hope of a Catholic upbringing.

2. **Can confirmation or first communion be delayed after an older child has been baptized?**

Sometimes an older child receives the sacrament of baptism. Such a child has reached "catechetical age." The *Rite of Christian Initiation for Children Who Have Reached Catechetical Age* states that such children are capable of "receiving and nurturing a personal faith and of recognizing an obligation of conscience" (#252). For the narrow and explicit purposes of Christian initiation, children who have reached the age of reason are considered adults (CIC 852 §1, CCEO 681 §3). Their formation should follow the same pattern as that of adults, appropriately adapted to their age. They should receive the sacraments of baptism, confirmation, and Eucharist at the Easter Vigil. It would not be appropriate for a pastoral minister, after baptizing a child who is of catechetical age, to delay either first reception of the Eucharist or confirmation to a later time for the purpose of including the child in a parish first communion or confirmation "program."

3. **Can a diocese establish a policy for the reception of confirmation before first holy communion?**

Many dioceses in the United States are implementing the "Restored Order of the Sacraments of Initiation" in which the sacraments of Christian initiation are received in the order in which they were first celebrated and received in the early Church: baptism, confirmation, and Eucharist. The RCIA requires that these three sacraments be received together and it seems also appropriate that this order be observed for those baptized in infancy as Catholics. This arrangement affirms confirmation as the strengthening and completion of baptism and allows Eucharist to culminate the initiation process and express full membership in the Catholic Church.

In accordance with c. 891, confirmation is to be celebrated around the age of discretion (around seven years), unless the conference of bishops has decided otherwise. The USCCB has designated the age of confirmation to be between the age of discretion and age sixteen. Each local bishop determines for his diocese the particular age from within that range.

4. **Can cohabiting Catholic couples be denied the sacrament of marriage?**

Several rights coalesce in the issue of cohabiting couples seeking to marry in the Church, a situation that has become much more prevalent in recent years. Canon 1058 (CCEO 778) states that all persons who are not prohibited by law can contract marriage. Canon 843 §1 (CCEO 381 §2) establishes that sacred ministers cannot refuse the sacraments to those who ask for them at appropriate times, are properly disposed, and are not prohibited by law from receiving them.

Many pastoral ministers sincerely believe that when couples live together before marriage, there is an indication that the couple is not properly disposed to celebrate the sacrament. *The Catechism of the Catholic Church*, in its description of "trial marriage," states that those who engage in premature sexual relations with the intention of getting married later enter a relationship that can "scarcely ensure mutual sincerity and fidelity. . . ." "Human love does not tolerate 'trial marriages.' It demands a total and definitive gift of persons to one another" (#2391).

Only an ordinary can legitimately prohibit the marriage of a couple within his jurisdiction, and only for a time, for a serious cause, and only as long as the cause persists (CIC 1077 §1, CCEO 794). Before the pastoral minister refers such a case to an ordinary, the marriage preparation required by CIC 1063 (CCEO 783, §1, §3) may well give the pastoral minister the opportunity to engage the couple in an extensive "teachable moment."

The Pontifical Council for the Family, in its document "Preparation for the Sacrament of Marriage," describes this evangelization as both a "maturation and deepening in the faith" (#2). It calls for an intense "remote preparation in which the family, school, and other groups with formation potential assist in the development of, and respect for, all authentic human values both in interpersonal and social relations, with all this implies for the formation of character, self-control, and self-esteem, the proper use of one's inclinations and respect for persons of the other sex" (#22).

5. Can the Christian faithful be denied the Church's funeral rites?

It sometimes happens that a request is made on behalf of the faithful departed for funeral rites in a parish in which the deceased was not an active participant. Canon 1177 §1 states that as a rule, funeral rites for any of the faithful departed are to be celebrated in his or her own parish church. However, any member of the faithful, or those commissioned to arrange for his or her funeral may choose another church for the funeral rites with the consent of the appropriate pastors (CIC 1177 §2).

Although canon 1184 permits the deprivation of funeral rites for those who are "manifest sinners" who do not show some sign of repentance and whose funeral rites would cause scandal, caution and pastoral care should be exercised. Such actions of denial require judgments about the spiritual state of certain individuals, as well as the possibility of causing serious damage to the faith of the surviving family. Many times, more scandal is caused to the ecclesial community by the denial of funeral rites than would be caused by the rites being celebrated in these questionable situations. As stated in the canon, in the situation of some doubt about the possibility of denial of funeral rites, the local ordinary is to be consulted and his judgment is to be followed.

6. **Can Catholics who serve in public office be denied the Eucharist for expressing opinions contrary to the Church's teaching?**

The general principles for admission to the Eucharist are provided in CIC 912. Baptized persons who are not prohibited by law can and must be admitted to holy communion. However, there are other canons which detail circumstances when a member of the Christian faithful is prohibited from receiving communion. For example, CIC 915 (CCEO 712) provides that "those who have been excommunicated or interdicted after the imposition or declaration of the penalty and others *obstinately persevering in manifest grave sin* are not to be admitted to holy communion. This canon restricts the free exercise of rights and is therefore, in virtue of CIC 18 (CCEO 1500), subject to strict interpretation.

For the restriction to apply when a person requests holy communion, four conditions must exist simultaneously (see F. G. Morrisey, "Denial of Access to the Sacraments" *CLSA Proceedings* 52(1990) pp. 170–186). The person must (1) be obstinate, (2) persist in the action, (3) be manifest, i.e., public and known, and (4) be seriously sinful. For a person to be considered "obstinate" there must have been an opportunity for admonitions, or warnings to the person about the situation.

The Christian faithful are bound by an obligation to always maintain communion with the Church (CIC 209, 223, CCEO 12, 26). A public position by a Catholic politician that is contrary to recognized Church teaching (e.g., abortion rights) could have the effect of disrupting ecclesial communion. The *Doctrinal Note on Some Questions Regarding the Participation of Catholics in Political Life* states:

> The Christian faith is an integral unity, and thus it is incoherent to isolate some particular elements to the detriment of the whole of Catholic doctrine. No Catholic can appeal to the principle of pluralism or to the autonomy of lay involvement in political life to support policies affecting the common good which compromise or undermine fundamental ethical requirements.
>
> CONGREGATION FOR THE DOCTRINE OF THE FAITH

One difficulty here lies in determining when a given action disrupts communion and goes against the common good, as well as discerning the best means to properly deal with the scenario.

Another right to be considered is provided in CIC 220 (CCEO 23): "No one is permitted to harm illegitimately the good reputation which a person possesses nor to injure the right of any person to protect his or her own privacy." When an individual is denied the sacraments it is possible to damage that person's reputation since they are identified to the community as a public sinner of some sort. Sometimes such an action (denial of the sacraments) has the reverse effect of "creating sympathy" for the person's opinion. Therefore, it is important that all the facts in each case are carefully assembled before denial of a sacrament takes place.

In July 2004, the U.S. Catholic Bishops issued a statement, "Catholics in Political Life," which addressed the issue of denial of communion to Catholic politicians. They said:

> Given the wide range of circumstances involved in arriving at a prudential judgment on a matter of this seriousness, we recognize that such decisions rest with the individual bishop in accord with established canonical and pastoral principles. Bishops can legitimately make different judgments on the most prudent course of pastoral action. Nevertheless, we all share an unequivocal commitment to protect human life and dignity and to preach the Gospel in difficult times.

Canon 1317 (CCEO 1636) states that "penalties are to be established only insofar as they are truly necessary to provide more suitably for ecclesiastical discipline." Therefore, the application of penalties should be, in the mind of the legislator, the "last step" in a delicate issue such as denial of a sacrament. It is presumed that appropriate discussion has taken place between the offending party and the Church official prior to the imposition of any penal actions.

7. What are the rights of bishops, priests, deacons, and the laity in the proper celebration of the liturgy?

The Roman Instruction *Redemptionis Sacramentum: On Certain Matters to Be Observed or to Be Avoided Regarding the Most Holy Eucharist* was issued on April 23, 2004, by the Congregation for Divine Worship and the Discipline of the Sacraments. It addressed several issues related to rights and the Eucharist. Included there is the right of Christ's faithful to a liturgical celebration that is an expression of the Church's life in accordance with her tradition and discipline

(# 11). The instruction further addresses the right of all of Christ's faithful to have the liturgy, and particularly the celebration of the Mass, be truly as the Church wishes, according to her stipulations as prescribed in the liturgical books and in the other laws and norms (# 12).

Canon 835 discusses the various roles of the ordained and laity in the celebration of the liturgy. Bishops are the principal dispensers of the mysteries of God and "directors, promoters and guardians of the entire liturgical life in the Church entrusted to them" (c. 835 §1). Presbyters are sharers of the priesthood of Christ and "under the authority of the bishop, they are consecrated to celebrate divine worship and to sanctify the people" (§2). Deacons also have a part in the celebration "according to the norm of the prescriptions of the law" (§3). The rest of the Christian faithful also have a role "by participating actively in their own way in liturgical celebrations, especially the Eucharist" (§4).

The supervision of the liturgy is entrusted to the authority of the Church residing in the Apostolic See and, where granted by the law, the diocesan bishop (c. 838 §1). More specifically, it is the responsibility of several different authoritative bodies within the Church.

The apostolic see has the right and obligation:
+ to order the sacred liturgy
+ to publish the liturgical books
+ to review their translations into the vernacular
+ to see to it that liturgical norms are faithfully observed (CIC 838 §2, CCEO 657 §2).

The episcopal conferences are given the right and responsibility of
+ preparing the translations of liturgical rites into the vernacular language with the appropriate adaptations within the limits given in the liturgical books themselves

- then publishing the rites after review by the Holy See (CIC 838 §3, CCEO 657 §3).

The diocesan bishop has the right to

- issue appropriate liturgical norms, within his competence, for his diocese (CIC 838 §4, CCEO 657 §4).

The Christian faithful have the right

- to expect that their diocesan bishop takes care to prevent the occurrence of abuses in ecclesiastical discipline (*Redemptionis Sacramentum*, #24).

The Right of the Christian Faithful to Assemble

1. Are members of the Christian faithful permitted to organize and petition for changes in Church structure or teaching?

Members of the Christian faithful, since they participate in the mission of the Church, are at liberty to freely govern associations for charitable and religious purposes (CIC 215, CCEO 18). The Christian faithful also have the right to make known their needs and desires to their pastors (CIC 212 §2, CCEO 15). In addition,

> according to the knowledge, competence, and prestige which they possess, they have the right and even at times the duty to manifest to the sacred pastors their opinion on matters which pertain to the good of the Church and to make their opinion known to the rest of the Christian faithful. . . . (CIC 212 §3, CCEO 15)

This right must always be exercised with due regard for the integrity of the faith and morals, and with "reverence toward their pastors, and attentive to common advantage and the dignity of persons" (CIC 212 §3, CCEO 15). It must also be kept in mind, in accordance with CIC 209 §1 (CCEO

12), that the Christian faithful "even in their own manner of acting, are always obliged to maintain communion with the Church." Ecclesiastical authority, for the protection of the common good, has the competence to regulate the exercise of the rights that belong to the Christian faithful (CIC 223 §2, CCEO 26).

2. May the Christian faithful publicly express dissent from Church teachings?

A distinction should be made concerning the expression of opinion, the right addressed in CIC 212 (CCEO 15), and the expression of dissent from official teaching. Canon 752 (CCEO 599) speaks of a religious respect of intellect and will that is to be paid to the teachings which the pope or the College of Bishops enunciate on faith or morals when they exercise the authentic magisterium "even if they do not intend to proclaim it by definitive act." Such a response on the part of the Christian faithful underscores a healthy respect and acceptance of sound teaching in the Church.

Canon 753 (CCEO 600) states that the bishops individually or when gathered in conferences of bishops or particular councils, and in communion with the head and members of the episcopal college, are authentic teachers of the faith. The faithful must adhere to the authentic teaching of their own bishops "with religious submission."

There is a recognized complementary relationship with the bishops that theologians exercise in their efforts to study and reflect on the teachings of the Church. *Doctrinal Responsibilities: Approaches to Promoting Cooperation and Resolving Misunderstandings between Bishops and Theologians,* approved and published by the National Conference of Catholic Bishops on June 17, 1989, should be consulted as a guide that emphasizes informal cooperation in the Church's teaching mission. This document proposes the resolution of disputes concerning doctrinal issues in an informal manner and conversational manner.

The Patrimony of the Church

1. May parishioners hold title to the assets of a parish?

The Catholic Church, while being a spiritual reality, is also a material entity, dependent on secular means of commerce and transactions to accomplish its ministry in the world. The Church utilizes various legal institutes to assist in its mission. In addition to "physical" persons—individuals who are baptized and therefore subject to rights and duties—the *Code of Canon Law* also makes reference to "juridic" persons. Somewhat analogous to civil "corporations" in the secular realm, juridic persons, such as a parish or a diocese, are also subject to rights and obligations. Juridic persons are established in order to accomplish the work of the Church, which at times transcends any one individual. The competent legislator in the Church brings juridic persons into existence, and can suppress them, if ever need be.

Canon 1256 (CCEO 1008 §2) states: "Under the supreme authority of the Roman Pontiff, ownership of goods belongs to that juridic person which has acquired them legitimately." The parish is a juridic person, since it is created to serve the people of God beyond the tenure of pastors and the first parishioners. Its temporal goods do not belong to the pastor or the community; rather they belong to the parish. The pastor and the community, however, are to administer the goods exercising good stewardship.

The temporal goods which belong to the Church (universal, diocesan, or parish) are "ecclesiastical goods" (goods that belong to a properly erected juridic person of the Church) and must be regulated by canon law as well as by the approved statutes of the juridic person. By virtue of CIC

532 (CCEO 290 §1), the pastor represents the parish in all juridic affairs in accord with the norms of law. He is to see to it that the parish goods are administered in accord with the provisions of the code (CIC 1281–1288, CCEO 1024–1032). However, he is also to be assisted by a finance council, a mandatory consultative body that is regulated by universal and diocesan law (CIC 537, CCEO 295). In this council, Christian faithful "assist the pastor in the administration of the goods of the parish. . . ."

2. May parishioners overrule a decision by a bishop to close a parish?

There has been a sharp decline in the number of priests available to serve in ministry over the last several years. This has forced many bishops to make painful decisions about closing parishes. Dioceses utilize a variety of means to determine which, if any, parishes to close. Sometimes several parishes are merged into one, or a pastor and a pastoral staff jointly serve several parishes. Using CIC 517 §2, a bishop, due to the dearth of priests, may assign the pastoral care of a parish to a deacon or another person while appointing a priest with the powers and faculties of a pastor to supervise the pastoral care.

Even with such efforts to staff parishes, it sometimes becomes inevitable that for a variety of reasons, a parish must be closed. Canon 515 §2 (CCEO 280 §2) establishes that the diocesan bishop is competent to "erect, suppress, or notably alter parishes." However, before undertaking the notable change of a parish he is first to hear the presbyteral council, the body of priests representing the priests of the diocese, who aid the bishop in his governance of the diocese. This council, when advising the bishop in the matter of a notable alteration in a parish, should be well informed with appropriate documentation so the members can provide informed counsel. Ultimately, however, the bishop is competent to establish, close, or alter a parish after the appropriate consultation.

A parishioner who wishes to challenge such a decision by the bishop may lodge recourse against the decree of closure or "suppression" (See chapter 6). Such a procedure requests that the bishop alters, rescinds, or changes his decision and must be undertaken within certain prescribed time limits. If the original decision is not changed, the complainant then has the option of appealing to the Holy See.

The Rights of Employment in the Church

1. May members of the Christian faithful form or join labor unions?

There is no specific mention of labor unions in the *Code of Canon Law*. However, the Christian faithful, in CIC 215 (CCEO 8) have the right to freely found and direct associations for the purpose of the promotion of the Christian vocation in the world. Pope John Paul II, in his encyclical *Laborem Exercens, On Human Work* (1981), draws on the teachings that have reiterated the value of labor associations, particularly Pope Leo XIII's *Rerum Novarum*. John Paul writes:

> All these rights [just wages and work benefits], together with the need for the workers themselves to secure them, give rise to yet another right: the right of association, that is to form associations for the purpose of defending the vital interests of those employed in the various professions. These associations are called labor or trade unions. (*Laborem Exercens*, #20.1)

John Paul warned that the efforts of such associations should always take into account the limitations imposed by the general economic situation of the country. Workers must also be careful in the use of strikes or work stoppages that they never be abused, especially for political purposes.

2. What are the employment rights and obligations of those employed by the Church for service and ministry?

Lay persons who devote themselves permanently or even temporarily to some special service to the Church are obliged to acquire the appropriate formation which is required to fulfill their functions properly and to carry them out conscientiously, zealously, and diligently (CIC 231 §1, CCEO 409). They have a right to a decent remuneration, so that they may, like all members of the Christian faithful, be able to provide decently for their own needs and for those of their family (CIC 231 §2, CCEO 409). Canon 1286 (CCEO 1030) requires that those who administer goods in the name of the Church "are to observe meticulously the civil laws pertaining to labor and social policy according to Church principles in the employment of workers." It further specifies that the administrators "are to pay a just and decent wage to employees so they are able to provide fittingly for their own needs and those of their dependents."

The Church has often taught that the justice of a socioeconomic system can be evaluated by examining whether or not the worker's labor is properly remunerated (See for example, John Paul II, *Laborem Exercens*, no. 19). The Church, before teaching ethics related to labor, must first be sure that it is practicing its own teachings in this matter internally, especially in regard to those who have devoted themselves to its service.

3. Do those who work in church ministries have a right to employment benefits and pension?

With due regard for CIC 231 §1 (CCEO 409) which addresses the obligation of receiving proper training and formation for specialized service, those who labor for the

Church also have a right that retirement savings, social security, and health benefits are duly provided for. This is to be done with due regard for the prescriptions of civil law (CIC 231 §2, CCEO 409).

> Within the sphere of these principal rights, there develops a whole system of particulàr rights which, together with remuneration for work, determine the correct relationship between worker and employer. (*Laborem Exercens*, no. 19.6)

The National Association of Church Personnel Administrators (NACPA) has prepared a helpful position paper, *Just Treatment for Those Who Work for the Church*, that outlines a comprehensive approach to issues affecting the wide variety of church workers. Included in these principles is one that states that church-related institutions that have "functioned as a prophetic voice in calling societies and governments to the practice of justice, [. . .] should model just treatment for all persons working for them" (p. 11). Such institutions are invited by this document to consider, among several ethical principles, personnel policies that are compatible with the mission and values of the Church and the implementation of the principle of subsidiarity where applicable.

The Rights of Clergy

1. When may a pastor be removed from a parish by the bishop? What legal procedures must be followed?

If a pastor has been appointed legitimately to a term of office and the term has expired, the pastor can be lawfully reassigned to another parish by the diocesan bishop. When the ministry of a pastor has become detrimental or ineffective for any reason, even if it is not due to any grave cause of his own making, he can be removed from the parish by the diocesan bishop (CIC 1740, CCEO 1389).

Canon 1741 (CCEO 1390) mentions five reasons that could prompt such an action:

1. A way of acting which is gravely detrimental or disturbing to the ecclesial community.
2. Incompetence or a permanent infirmity of mind or body that renders the pastor incapable of performing his duties.
3. Loss of good reputation among upright and good parishioners or some aversion to the pastor by the parishioners which is foreseen as lasting for some time.
4. Grave neglect or violation of parochial duties which continues after a warning.
5. Poor administration of the temporal affairs of the parish with grave damage to the Church which cannot be handled in any other way.

The bishop, in order to remove the pastor, must carefully observe the procedure for removal contained in CIC 1740–1747 (CCEO 1389–1396). These procedures include:

1. An inquiry.
2. The bishop discussing the situation with two pastors from a group permanently selected for this by the presbyteral council from a list nominated by the bishop.
3. The bishop paternally persuading the pastor to resign the pastorate within a period of fifteen days, with the reasons and arguments for removal.
4. The bishop repeating his invitation for the pastor's resignation.

If the pastor refuses to respond within the time limit or refuses to resign with no reason offered, the bishop may issue a decree of removal. If the pastor opposes the causes alleged for removal and gives reasons for remaining which seem insufficient to the bishop, the bishop invites the pastor to prepare a defense in a written report and to offer proofs to the contrary.

The bishop must allow the pastor to review the acts of the case that have been prepared against him. The bishop must consider the matter with the same two priests selected from the presbyteral council and then finally determine whether the pastor must be removed, promptly issuing a decree on the matter. The bishop must provide for the removed priest with an assignment to another office (if he is suitable for this) or through a pension as the case requires and circumstances permit. Should the priest decide to make a formal appeal to the Holy See against his removal, the bishop may not appoint a new pastor, but instead must appoint a parish administrator who assumes pastoral care for the parish until the case is resolved.

There is no similar procedure required for the removal from office of a parochial vicar (associate pastor). However, the general norms of the Church state that for removal from office, such a decision should be in writing and with the reason(s) provided (CIC 193 §4; CCEO 974 §2).

2. **What rights are accorded to those who make allegations of sexual misconduct against a cleric? What obligations do they have?**

Several rights that belong to the Christian faithful apply in the unfortunate situation of an allegation of sexual abuse by a cleric (see *Revised Guide to the Implementation of the U.S. Bishops Essential Norms for Diocesan/Eparchial Policies Dealing with Allegations of Sexual Abuse of Minors By Priests or Deacons;* Canon Law Society of America, 2004).

1. An individual (or a parent or guardian, in the case of a minor) who believes that they have been sexually abused by a cleric has the right to make known his or her complaint to the Church. This is in accordance with CIC 212 (CCEO 15): the "Christian faithful are

free to make known to the pastors of the Church their needs, especially spiritual ones, and their desires."

2. They also have the right "to receive assistance from the sacred pastors out of the spiritual goods of the Church" (CIC 213, CCEO 16).

3. Individuals who make an accusation have the right to expect that their good name and reputation will be protected as the procedure used to determine the accuracy of the allegation unfolds (CIC 220, CCEO 23).

4. The individual has a right to have the procedures and processes that have been designated in such instances followed and properly observed (see CIC 221, CCEO 24).

5. The individual also has a right to pursue recourse if they believe that their rights in pursuing the complaint have not been observed (see chapter 6). A competent canonist should be consulted for assistance in initiating formal recourse.

3. What rights are accorded to clerics accused of sexual misconduct? What obligations do they have?

The cleric against whom allegations have been made is also subject to various rights and obligations.

1. Foremost, he has the right granted all members of the Christian faithful "not to be punished with canonical penalties except according to the norm of law" (CIC 221 §3 CCEO 24).

2. He has the legitimate right to have the proper procedures followed. These include the right of self-defense and the assistance of a canonical advocate (See United States Conference of Catholic Bishops, *Promise to Protect, Pledge to Heal: Charter for the*

Protection of Children and Young People and Essential Norms, 2003).

3. As a member of the Christian faithful, the accused cleric also enjoys the right of confidentiality and to a good reputation while the processes for determination of his guilt or innocence take place (CIC 220, CCEO 23).

4. The right of privacy is also to be observed in the case of medical and/or psychological evaluations to be utilized for the accused. A cleric cannot be impelled to undergo psychological testing or treatment against his will.

4. What are the rights and obligations of a bishop in dealing with an accusation of sexual offense against a minor by a member of the clergy?

The bishop has the most serious obligation to protect children and young people from sexual abuse by clerics. In the last several years, the U.S. bishops have taken measures to put in place various policies that reach out to those who have made allegations, as well as to their families. They have committed themselves to their spiritual and emotional well-being, whether the abuse was recent or occurred many years ago. (See *Promise to Protect, Pledge to Heal: Charter for the Protection of Children and Young People* and *Essential Norms,* 2003). This solicitude includes each diocese establishing a formal outreach program for every person who has been the victim of sexual abuse, with the provisions of counseling, spiritual assistance, support groups, and various other social services. The bishop and/or his delegate will meet with such victims and listen to them with compassion. The bishops have also committed themselves to responding promptly when such allegations are made.

The bishops have the right and obligation:

1. to use the procedures that have been established by universal law, the norms of the episcopal conference and particular law to determine the validity of an accusation.

2. to follow through with appropriate penalties if warranted.

3. to protect the rights of all parties involved.

The Right to a Catholic Education

1. Must parents provide a Catholic education for their children?

Canon 226 §2 (CCEO 627 §1) is quite clear regarding the serious responsibility of parents to provide for the Christian education of their children, "according to the doctrine handed on by the Church." The Church unequivocally recognizes and supports the work of Catholic schools which embody "an educational philosophy in which faith, culture and life are brought into harmony" (Congregation for Catholic Education, *The Religious Dimension of Education in a Catholic School*, 1988). Catholic schools are undoubtedly important in the life of the Catholic community. Still, because the Church recognizes the family as the basic unit of society and of the Church, it leaves parents free to determine the particular method of Catholic education:

> Catholic parents also have the duty and right of choosing those means and institutions through which they can provide more suitably for the Catholic education of their children, according to local circumstances (CIC 793 §1, CCEO 627 §2).

> When parents are unable to provide Catholic school education for their children, they are

obliged to make sure that suitable Catholic education is provided for their children outside the schools. (CIC 798, CCEO 633 §2)

2. Who decides when a child is properly prepared to receive a sacrament?

The canons direct attention to the responsibility of parents for the Christian formation of their children, which includes preparation for the reception of the sacraments of the Church. The *Declaration on Christian Education* states:

> Since parents have conferred life on their children, they have a most solemn obligation to educate their offspring. Hence parents must be acknowledged as the first and foremost educators of their children. (GE #3)

Canon 914, in addressing preparation of children for first communion states:

> It is primarily the duty of the parents and those who take the place of parents as well as of the duty of pastors to take care that children who have reached the use of reason are prepared properly. . . .

The law envisions a close collaboration between the parents and the pastor (or his delegate) in determining the readiness of a child to receive the sacrament. The emphasis upon the role of the parents flows naturally from their responsibility in being the primary teachers of their children in the ways of faith.

CHAPTER 6

Vindicating Rights in the Church

Due Process

The law of the Catholic Church encourages its members to avoid contention and to settle differences in a peaceful manner (see CIC 1446 §1, CCEO 1103). This is addressed even more specifically in CIC 1659 §1 (CCEO 1345), which states that the infliction of penalties is always to be seen as "the last resort," when all other attempts to resolve a matter of discipline have failed. Efforts to resolve disputes within the Church should begin by using due process. In this way, the gospel injunction as outlined in Matthew 18:15–17 is honored.

> If your brother should commit some wrong against you, go and point out his fault but keep it between the two of you. If he listens to you, you have won your brother. If he does not listen, summon another, so that every case may stand on the word of two or three witnesses. If he ignores them, refer it to the Church.

Two appropriate means of dispute resolution are the utilization of *conciliation* and *arbitration*. Conciliation involves a neutral party attempting to mediate a conflict by bringing the parties involved to a mutually acceptable and satisfactory resolution concerning the issue(s) in dispute.

In arbitration, the mediator—by mutual decision of the disputing parties—creates a binding agreement prepared by the arbiter after working with the disputants. The parties agree beforehand to accept the eventual resolution that will be formed by the arbiter.

The United States Conference of Catholic Bishops has left the establishment of such processes to the discretion of the individual diocesan bishop. Some dioceses have created departments or offices whose responsibility it is to make available due process for any individual who believes a canonical right has been violated. Often such offices are available to resolve employment issues, whether they be parish or diocesan-related. Even if a formal canonical recourse has been initiated, conciliation and arbitration can be used as an appropriate alternative.

The Archdiocese of Milwaukee has been a strong proponent of due process dispute resolution. The procedures used have been widely accepted by the members of the archdiocese and have been implemented for several years to deal effectively with a variety of disputes. It is offered here as one particular model that might be considered by other dioceses, in whole or in part, to help promote the gospel value of reconciliation when controversies arise.

Dispute Resolution in the Archdiocese of Milwaukee

The Process

1. A conflict arises on a local level, most commonly a parish, e.g., between a pastor and a parish council over an issue on which the pastor and council cannot agree. According to the norms of the archdiocese, each parish is to have a trained "grievance committee" that hears the matter and offers to mediate the issue between the parties.

2. If the issue cannot be resolved at this level, the matter can be appealed to the appropriate archdiocesan agency or department. Each agency and department is required to have a due process procedure and to utilize this procedure as needed.

3. If the appropriate archdiocesan agency or department is unable to resolve the issue, it is referred to the archdiocesan due process office. This office carefully reviews and screens the petition to make sure the prior attempts at conciliation have been applied appropriately.

4. An "Archdiocesan Court of Equity" has been established in the Archdiocese to hear disputes and resolve contentious matters. Should the archdiocesan due process office be unable to bring the matter to resolution, the disputant may petition the Court of Equity for a hearing. Each side of the dispute is provided with a list of approved canonical advocates and judge(s) are appointed to hear the matter. After the issues are appropriately clarified, a hearing is scheduled where the "Oral Contentious Process" outlined in canons CIC 1656–1670 (CCEO 1343–1356) is used. At the end of the hearing, the judge(s) renders a judgment and, if appropriate, also assesses damages and costs. Should, for example, a member of the Christian faithful believe that his or her reputation has been unlawfully damaged (CIC 220, CCEO 23), the appropriate route would be a judicial trial.

5. If either party does not accept this decision, they may appeal the matter to the archbishop. The archbishop would be provided all the relevant information about the case and would render his decision in the matter.

6. Should either party still feel aggrieved, they may appeal the issue to the appropriate dicastery (administrative office) of the Holy See.

Advantages

1. The most obvious advantage is that it effectively promotes resolution of a conflicting matter, rather than letting an issue simmer and perhaps ultimately become even more destructive to the local community. It follows the instructions given by Jesus in Matthew to resolve controversies by mediation, with different stages or levels.
2. It also has the advantage of beginning at the local level. (See #1 above.)
3. It recognizes that controversies and disagreements in any society of human beings are inevitable. Having a trained parish grievance board available not only acknowledges this reality, but teaches important skills that can be utilized in a variety of settings.
4   It also shows clearly that not every contentious issue that arises in a parish setting needs to be resolved by the (arch) diocese or by the bishop directly.

Disadvantages

1. The process presupposes training at the various levels of appeal, including the parish. This necessarily implies time, effort, and possible expenses. At the local level, the parish would pay this cost. While many will see this as a good investment, others will not.
2. There exists also the possibility that parties to a dispute, aware that the end of the process may involve a review by the diocesan bishop and ultimately the Holy See, may decide to obfuscate or refuse to come to a resolution of the matter until it comes to a superior. The

only effective means to deal with this possibility is for parties to enter into due process in good faith.

Utilizing a process such as this for resolving disputes means having in place well-trained individuals who are familiar with both the processes and human nature at every stage of the process. It also means offering good incentives for coming to an acceptable resolution of the matter.

Hierarchical Recourse in the Catholic Church

In resolving disputes, the Church often uses a procedure known as "hierarchical recourse." This procedure is used when an individual believes that he or she has been injured by a decision made by a Church authority. The complainant, if not satisfied with a decision given by a church authority, attempts to appeal that decision to that person's "hierarchic superior." For example, if a member of the Christian faithful believes his or her rights have been violated by a diocesan bishop, the appeal is made to the appropriate congregation in Rome. If the complainant does not know the appropriate congregation to address concerning the matter, the law provides that the complaint may be given to the author of the disputed decree, who must "transmit it immediately to the competent hierarchical superior" (CIC 1737 §1, CCEO 997 §1).

The act that has injured the party must be in the form of a decree, or a written communication that describes a decision by a Church authority. With this documentation in hand, the aggrieved party can seek canonical redress in an effort to vindicate his or her rights. However, before utilizing this procedure, certain conditions must be verified:

Conditions

1. The act that is being challenged must be in conformity with the understanding of the code. CIC 35 (CCEO 1510 §1) states, "A singular administrative

act, whether it is a decree, a precept, or a rescript, can be issued by one who possesses executive power within the limits of that person's competence. . . ."

2. CIC 48 (CCEO 1510 §2,1°) describes a singular decree as an "administrative act issued by a competent executive authority, whereby in accordance with the norms of law a decision is given or a provision made for a particular case."

3. Contrary to many forms of government such as the American model that separates legislative, executive, and judicial functions, the Church invests diocesan bishops with all three responsibilities. Diocesan bishops (and those equivalent to them by law) exercise executive authority and are capable of issuing administrative acts. Others who exercise executive power include vicars general and episcopal vicars.

Before beginning recourse, it is important that the decree that has been issued fulfills all the above requirements; i.e., it is the result of a discretionary administrative act, it is in the form of a decree, and it has been properly executed by a person who legitimately exercises executive authority. It would also be important to establish that the person who issued the decree has competence (e.g., they were acting in their own particular territory, so that they had proper jurisdiction), and that there is nothing in the particular subject matter being addressed that might affect the validity of the action even before the aggrieved party makes formal recourse.

A recourse against an administrative act takes place within several stages. The procedure and its component parts must be carefully observed. In many instances, failure to comply with an individual step of the procedure can nullify the entire recourse.

The Procedure

1. **A written request must be made by the aggrieved party seeking from the person who issued the decree one of the following:**

   ◆ a request that the original decree be revoked;

   ◆ a request that the original decree be somehow changed or amended (CIC 1734 §1, CCEO 999).

   Such a request may be helpful in bringing the issuing authority the knowledge, previously unknown, that a person feels aggrieved over a decision that has been rendered. It also provides the issuing authority the opportunity to review the circumstances that led to the decree and the possibility of changing the outcome by revising or even revoking the original decree. Such notification is in keeping with the desire of the law for amicable resolutions.

2. **The person making the challenge must do so within ten "useful" or "available" days after receiving notification of the decree (CIC 1734 §2, CCEO 999).**

   CIC 201 §2 (CCEO 1544 §2) describes "useful time" as the time that a person has to exercise a right. Some commentators understand this time period running continuously, but excluding a holiday if it occurs on the last day in which a person may act.

3. **If the author of the decree being challenged is directly responsible to the bishop, the recourse is made directly to the diocesan bishop (CIC 1734 §3, CCEO 999).**

4. **The issuing authority has thirty days to respond to the request by the petitioner to modify or amend the original decree (CIC 1735).**

After receiving the petition, the issuing authority has three options:

1. Revoke original decree
2. Amend the original decree in some manner
3. Ignore the decree and not respond

The issuing authority has thirty days to respond should it be decided that the decree will be revoked or modified. The days are computed as "continuous days."

If the author of the decree does not respond within thirty days, or if the aggrieved party is still not satisfied with the response of the issuing authority, the petitioner may appeal directly to the hierarchical superior of the decree's author; i.e., to the appropriate Roman congregation.

5. Suspension of the decree (CIC 1736, CCEO 1000).

Sometimes, appropriate to the subject matter, the original decree that has been appealed to Rome has its effects suspended until the case is decided. The author of the decree can decide to suspend the effects of the decree voluntarily. If the author does not suspend the effects of the decree within ten days, the petitioner is free to request suspension from the hierarchic superior (Roman Congregation).

6. The recourse can be transmitted directly to the Roman Congregation or sent to the author of the decree for immediate transmittal to the appropriate Congregation (CIC 1737 §1, CCEO 997).

The person appealing to Rome should state the reasons for the recourse, along with appropriate documentation, including the issue of possible damages. The appeal must be made within fifteen useful days. The time runs from the day the response was given or after the thirty day time limit by the author of the decree expired.

Ordinarily, the Congregation will communicate with the bishop whose decision is being challenged, asking for a response. The Congregation may also invite the complainant to submit more details or information concerning the case. Since this is not a judicial process, there is no debate or hearing of arguments between the complainant and the bishop by the Congregation. The Congregation, in accordance with CIC 1733 §3 (CCE0 998), may seek to resolve the issue by an equitable solution, for example, by using mediation.

7. **Those seeking to make recourse have the right to be assisted by an advocate (CIC 1738, CCEO 1003).**

It is recommended that a canonical advocate familiar with administrative recourse be utilized in undertaking formal recourse procedures. Dioceses and religious communities should carefully consider subsidizing an advocate with the hope that a more equitable solution is obtained when both sides in a dispute have canonical representation.

8. **The hierarchic superior may respond to the recourse in one of several different ways:**
   1. Confirm the original decree
   2. Declare the act invalid due to some violation of law
   3. Order rescinding or revocation of the original decree
   4. Amend the original decree
   5. Replace the original decree with one of its own
   6. Issue a new decree contrary to the original one. (See CIC 1739, CCEO 1004)

9. **If there is no response by the Congregation within three months, or if the complainant or the bishop has been notified by the Congregation of its decision in the matter, the case can be appealed to the next hierarchical level, the Apostolic Signatura, within thirty available days (PB 123).**

However, the Congregation is entitled to extend this time limit if it believes that due to the complexity of the case, more time is needed. The Congregation must then inform the complainant.

10. **The complainant to the Signatura may seek recourse against what is believed to be violation(s) of the law or against the procedures used by the Congregation in making its decision.**

Thus the Signatura, if it decides that a particular decision was in violation of the law, could nullify the Congregation's action in the matter that had been challenged. If the Congregation had supported or affirmed the bishop's decision, the Congregation's own decision could also be nullified. The complainant may also then request damages to be awarded by the Signatura.

11. **Recourse to the Signatura does not automatically suspend the previous decision of the Congregation (unless the universal law of the Church states otherwise).**

CIC 1629 1° (CCEO 1310 1°) states that there is no appeal from a sentence of the Apostolic Signatura. However, a complaint of nullity (that seeks to establish the sentence is null for a reason given in law) can be entered or the complainant may seek to have a retrial.

THE CANONS

Listed below are the canons that enumerate the various rights of the People of God as found in the *Code of Canon Law* (1983). The corresponding canons of the *Code of Canons of the Eastern Churches* are not provided, since in most cases they duplicate the Latin code.

The Obligations and Rights of All the Christian Faithful

CAN. 208 From their rebirth in Christ, there exists among all the Christian faithful a true equality regarding dignity and action by which they all cooperate in the building up of the Body of Christ according to each one's own condition and function.

CAN. 209

§1. The Christian faithful, even in their own manner of acting, are always obliged to maintain communion with the Church.

§2. With great diligence they are to fulfill the duties which they owe to the universal Church and the particular church to which they belong according to the prescripts of the law.

CAN. 210 All the Christian faithful must direct their efforts to lead a holy life and to promote the growth of the Church and its continual sanctification, according to their own condition.

CAN. 211 All the Christian faithful have the duty and right to work so that the divine message of salvation more and more reaches all people in every age and in every land.

CAN. 212

§1. Conscious of their own responsibility, the Christian faithful are bound to follow with Christian obedience those things which the sacred pastors, inasmuch as they represent Christ, declare as teachers of the faith or establish as rulers of the Church.

§2. The Christian faithful are free to make known to the pastors of the Church their needs, especially spiritual ones, and their desires.

§3. According to the knowledge, competence, and prestige which they possess, they have the right and even at times the duty to manifest to the sacred pastors their opinion on matters which pertain to the good of the Church and to make their opinion known to the rest of the Christian faithful, without prejudice to the integrity of faith and morals, with reverence toward their pastors, and attentive to common advantage and the dignity of persons.

CAN. 213 The Christian faithful have the right to receive assistance from the sacred pastors out of the spiritual goods of the Church, especially the word of God and the sacraments.

CAN. 214 The Christian faithful have the right to worship God according to the prescripts of their own rite approved by the legitimate pastors of the Church and to follow their own form of spiritual life so long as it is consonant with the doctrine of the Church.

CAN. 215 The Christian faithful are at liberty freely to found and direct associations for purposes of charity or piety or for the promotion of the Christian vocation in the world and to hold meetings for the common pursuit of these purposes.

CAN. 216 Since they participate in the mission of the Church, all the Christian faithful have the right to promote or sustain apostolic action even by their own undertakings, according to their own state and condition. Nevertheless, no undertaking is to claim the name *Catholic* without the consent of competent ecclesiastical authority.

CAN. 217 Since they are called by baptism to lead a life in keeping with the teaching of the gospel, the Christian faithful have the right to a Christian education by which they are to be instructed properly to strive for the maturity of the human person and at the same time to know and live the mystery of salvation.

CAN. 218 Those engaged in the sacred disciplines have a just freedom of inquiry and of expressing their opinion prudently on those matters in which they possess expertise, while observing the submission due to the magisterium of the Church.

CAN. 219 All the Christian faithful have the right to be free from any kind of coercion in choosing a state of life.

CAN. 220 No one is permitted to harm illegitimately the good reputation which a person possesses nor to injure the right of any person to protect his or her own privacy.

CAN. 221

§1. The Christian faithful can legitimately vindicate and defend the rights which they possess in the Church in the competent ecclesiastical forum according to the norm of law.

§2. If they are summoned to a trial by a competent authority, the Christian faithful also have the right to be judged according to the prescripts of the law applied with equity.

§3. The Christian faithful have the right not to be punished with canonical penalties except according to the norm of law.

CAN. 222

§l. The Christian faithful are obliged to assist with the needs of the Church so that the Church has what is necessary for divine worship, for the works of the apostolate and of charity, and for the decent support of ministers.

§2. They are also obliged to promote social justice and, mindful of the precept of the Lord, to assist the poor from their own resources.

CAN. 223

§l. In exercising their rights, the Christian faithful, both as individuals and gathered together in associations, must take into account the common good of the Church, the rights of others, and their own duties toward others.

§2. In view of the common good, ecclesiastical authority can direct the exercise of rights which are proper to the Christian faithful.

The Obligations and Rights of the Lay Christian Faithful

CAN. 224 In addition to those obligations and rights which are common to all the Christian faithful and those which are established in other canons, the lay Christian faithful are bound by the obligations and possess the rights which are enumerated in the canons of this title.

CAN. 225

§1. Since, like all the Christian faithful, lay persons are designated by God for the apostolate through baptism and confirmation, they are bound by the general obligation and possess the right as individuals, or joined in associations, to work so that the divine message of salvation is made known and accepted by all persons everywhere in the world. This obligation is even more compelling in those circumstances in which only through them can people hear the gospel and know Christ.

§2. According to each one's own condition, they are also bound by a particular duty to imbue and perfect the order of temporal affairs with the spirit of the gospel and thus to give witness to Christ, especially in carrying out these same affairs and in exercising secular functions.

CAN. 226

§1. According to their own vocation, those who live in the marital state are bound by a special duty to work through marriage and the family to build up the people of God.

§2. Since they have given life to their children, parents have a most grave obligation and possess the right to educate them. Therefore, it is for Christian parents particularly to take care of the Christian education of their children according to the doctrine handed on by the Church.

CAN. 227 The lay Christian faithful have the right to have recognized that freedom which all citizens have in the affairs of the earthly city. When using that same freedom, however, they are to take care that their actions are imbued with the spirit of the gospel and are to heed the doctrine set forth by the magisterium of the Church. In matters of opinion, moreover, they are to avoid setting forth their own opinion as the doctrine of the Church.

CAN. 228

§1. Lay persons who are found suitable are qualified to be admitted by the sacred pastors to those ecclesiastical offices and functions which they are able to exercise according to the precepts of the law.

§2. Lay persons who excel in necessary knowledge, prudence, and integrity are qualified to assist the pastors of the Church as experts and advisors, even in councils according to the norm of law.

CAN. 229

§l. Lay persons are bound by the obligation and possess the right to acquire knowledge of Christian doctrine appropriate to the capacity and condition of each in order for them to be able to live according to this doctrine, announce it themselves, defend it if necessary, and take their part in exercising the apostolate.

§2. They also possess the right to acquire that fuller knowledge of the sacred sciences which are taught in ecclesiastical universities and faculties or in institutes of religious sciences, by attending classes there and pursuing academic degrees.

§3. If the prescripts regarding the requisite suitability have been observed, they are also qualified to receive from legitimate ecclesiastical authority a mandate to teach the sacred sciences.

CAN. 230

§1. Lay men who possess the age and qualifications established by decree of the conference of bishops can be admitted on a stable basis through the prescribed liturgical rite to the ministries of lector and acolyte. Nevertheless, the conferral of these ministries does not grant them the right to obtain support or remuneration from the Church.

§2. Lay persons can fulfill the function of lector in liturgical actions by temporary designation. All lay persons can also perform the functions of commentator or cantor, or other functions, according to the norm of law.

§3. When the need of the Church warrants it and ministers are lacking, lay persons, even if they are not lectors or acolytes, can also supply certain of their duties, namely, to exercise the ministry of the word, to preside over liturgical prayers, to confer baptism, and to distribute Holy Communion, according to the prescripts of the law.

CAN. 231

§1. Lay persons who permanently or temporarily devote themselves to special service of the Church are obliged to acquire the appropriate formation required to fulfill their function properly and to carry out this function conscientiously, eagerly, and diligently.

§2. Without prejudice to the prescript of Can. 230, §1 and with the prescripts of civil law having been observed, lay persons have the right to decent remuneration appropriate to their condition so that they are able to provide decently for their own needs and those of their family. They also have a right for their social provision, social security, and health benefits to be duly provided.

The Obligations and Rights of Clerics

CAN. 273 Clerics are bound by a special obligation to show reverence and obedience to the Supreme Pontiff and their own ordinary.

CAN. 274

§1. Only clerics can obtain offices for whose exercise the power of orders or the power of ecclesiastical governance is required.

§2. Unless a legitimate impediment excuses them, clerics are bound to undertake and fulfill faithfully a function which their ordinary has entrusted to them.

CAN. 275

§1. Since clerics all work for the same purpose, namely, the building up of the Body of Christ, they are to be united among themselves by a bond of brotherhood and prayer and are to strive for cooperation among themselves according to the prescripts of particular law.

§2. Clerics are to acknowledge and promote the mission which the laity, each for his or her part, exercise in the Church and in the world.

CAN. 276

§1. In leading their lives, clerics are bound in a special way to pursue holiness since, having been consecrated to God by a new title in the reception of orders, they are dispensers of the mysteries of God in the service of His people.

§2. In order to be able to pursue this perfection:

1° they are first of all to fulfill faithfully and tirelessly the duties of the pastoral ministry;

2° they are to nourish their spiritual life from the two-fold table of sacred scripture and the Eucharist; therefore, priests are earnestly invited to offer the eucharistic sacrifice daily and deacons to participate in its offering daily;

3° priests and deacons aspiring to the presbyterate are obliged to carry out the liturgy of the hours daily according to the proper and approved liturgical books; permanent deacons, however, are to carry out the same to the extent defined by the conference of bishops;

4° they are equally bound to make time for spiritual retreats according to the prescripts of particular law;

5° they are urged to engage in mental prayer regularly, to approach the sacrament of penance frequently, to honor the Virgin Mother of God with particular veneration, and to use other common and particular means of sanctification.

CAN. 277

§1. Clerics are obliged to observe perfect and perpetual continence for the sake of the kingdom of heaven and therefore are bound to celibacy which is a special gift of God by which sacred ministers can adhere more easily to Christ with an undivided heart and are able to dedicate themselves more freely to the service of God and humanity.

§2. Clerics are to behave with due prudence towards persons whose company can endanger their obligation to observe continence or give rise to scandal among the faithful.

§3. The diocesan bishop is competent to establish more specific norms concerning this matter and to pass judgment in particular cases concerning the observance of this obligation.

CAN. 278

§1. Secular clerics have the right to associate with others to pursue purposes in keeping with the clerical state.

§2. Secular clerics are to hold in esteem especially those associations which, having statutes recognized by competent authority, foster their holiness in the exercise of the ministry through a suitable and properly approved rule of life and through fraternal assistance and which promote the unity of clerics among themselves and with their own bishop.

§3. Clerics are to refrain from establishing or participating in associations whose purpose or activity cannot be reconciled with the obligations proper to the clerical state or can prevent the diligent fulfillment of the function entrusted to them by competent ecclesiastical authority.

CAN. 279

§1. Even after ordination to the priesthood, clerics are to pursue sacred studies and are to strive after that solid doctrine founded in sacred scripture, handed on by their predecessors, and commonly accepted by the Church, as set out especially in the documents of councils and of the Roman Pontiffs. They are to avoid profane novelties and pseudo-science.

§2. According to the prescripts of particular law, priests are to attend pastoral lectures held after priestly ordination and, at times established by the same law, are also to attend other lectures, theological meetings, and conferences which offer them the opportunity to acquire a fuller knowledge of the sacred sciences and pastoral methods.

§3. They are also to acquire knowledge of other sciences, especially of those which are connected with the sacred sciences, particularly insofar as such knowledge contributes to the exercise of pastoral ministry.

CAN. 280 Some practice of common life is highly recommended to clerics; where it exists, it must be preserved as far as possible.

CAN. 281

§1. Since clerics dedicate themselves to ecclesiastical ministry, they deserve remuneration which is consistent with their condition, taking into account the nature of their function and the conditions of places and times, and by which they can provide for the necessities of their life as well as for the equitable payment of those whose services they need.

§2. Provision must also be made so that they possess that social assistance which provides for their needs suitably if they suffer from illness, incapacity, or old age.

§3. Married deacons who devote themselves completely to ecclesiastical ministry deserve remuneration by which they are able to provide for the support of themselves and their families. Those who receive remuneration by reason of a civil profession which they exercise or have exercised, however, are to take care of the needs of themselves and their families from the income derived from it.

CAN. 282

§1. Clerics are to foster simplicity of life and are to refrain from all things that have a semblance of vanity.

§2. They are to wish to use for the good of the Church and works of charity those goods which have come to them on the occasion of the exercise of ecclesiastical office and which are left over after provision has been made for their decent support and for the fulfillment of all the duties of their own state.

CAN. 283

§1. Even if clerics do not have a residential office, they nevertheless are not to be absent from their diocese for a notable period of time, to be determined by particular law, without at least the presumed permission of their proper ordinary.

§2. They are entitled, however, to a fitting and sufficient time of vacation each year as determined by universal or particular law.

CAN. 284 Clerics are to wear suitable ecclesiastical garb according to the norms issued by the conference of bishops and according to legitimate local customs.

CAN. 285

§1. Clerics are to refrain completely from all those things which are unbecoming to their state, according to the prescripts of particular law.

§2. Clerics are to avoid those things which, although not unbecoming, are nevertheless foreign to the clerical state.

§3. Clerics are forbidden to assume public offices which entail a participation in the exercise of civil power.

§4. Without the permission of their ordinary, they are not to take on the management of goods belonging to lay persons or secular offices which entail an obligation of rendering accounts. They are prohibited from giving surety even with their own goods without consultation with their proper ordinary. They also are to refrain from signing promissory notes, namely those through which they assume an obligation to make payment on demand.

CAN. 286 Clerics are prohibited from conducting business or trade personally or through others, for their own advantage or that of others, except with the permission of legitimate ecclesiastical authority.

CAN. 287

§l. Most especially, clerics are always to foster the peace and harmony based on justice which are to be observed among people.

§2. They are not to have an active part in political parties and in governing labor unions unless, in the judgment of competent ecclesiastical authority, the protection of the rights of the Church or the promotion of the common good requires it.

CAN. 288 The prescripts of Can. 284, 285, §§3 and 4, 286, and 287, §2 do not bind permanent deacons unless particular law establishes otherwise.

CAN. 289

§1. Since military service is hardly in keeping with the clerical state, clerics and candidates for sacred orders are not to volunteer for military service except with the permission of their ordinary.

§2. Clerics are to use exemptions from exercising functions and public civil offices foreign to the clerical state which laws and agreement or customs grant in their favor unless their proper ordinary has decided otherwise in particular cases.

HIERARCHIC RECOURSE AGAINST A DIOCESAN BISHOP

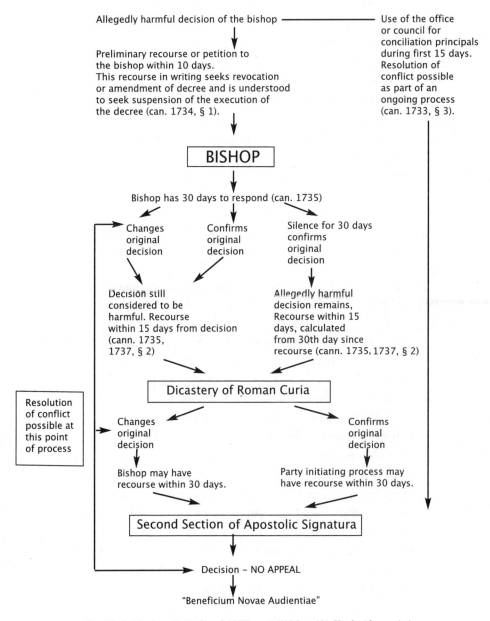

Allegedly harmful decision of the bishop ——————— Use of the office or council for conciliation principals during first 15 days. Resolution of conflict possible as part of an ongoing process (can. 1733, § 3).

Preliminary recourse or petition to the bishop within 10 days. This recourse in writing seeks revocation or amendment of decree and is understood to seek suspension of the execution of the decree (can. 1734, § 1).

BISHOP

Bishop has 30 days to respond (can. 1735)

Changes original decision

Confirms original decision

Silence for 30 days confirms original decision

Decision still considered to be harmful. Recourse within 15 days from decision (cann. 1735, 1737, § 2)

Allegedly harmful decision remains, Recourse within 15 days, calculated from 30th day since recourse (cann. 1735, 1737, § 2)

Dicastery of Roman Curia

Resolution of conflict possible at this point of process

Changes original decision

Confirms original decision

Bishop may have recourse within 30 days.

Party initiating process may have recourse within 30 days.

Second Section of Apostolic Signatura

Decision – NO APPEAL

"Beneficium Novae Audientiae"

Rev. Kevin Matthews in *Studia* vol. XVIII, no. 1 (1984), p. 231. Used with permission.

JUDICIAL TRIAL PROCEDURES

The Charter for the Protection of Children and Young People of the USCCB and its accompanying document, the *Essential Norms*, issued in 2002, attempt to outline an effective response to allegations of sexual abuse of a minor by a cleric. One measure that can be considered is a judicial penal procedure to impose the most serious church penalty, dismissal from the clerical state (permanent removal of a cleric from priestly or diaconal ministry). On April 30, 2001, a document approved by Pope John Paul II, *Sacramentorum sanctitatis tutela* (Safeguarding the Sanctity of the Sacraments) addressed, among several serious offenses, that of the sexual abuse of a minor by a cleric and outlined new procedures for bishops to deal with this crime.

The following is an outline of the canonical process that is followed in the penal procedure for the possible dismissal of a cleric from the clerical state:

1. When the bishop has completed the preliminary investigation and there seems sufficient indication that sexual abuse of a minor has occurred, he is to forward the data that has been collected, along with his *votum* (recommendations of the bishop/eparch concerning the case) to the Congregation for the Doctrine of the Faith in Rome.

2. The Congregation, after reviewing the case, will then decide whether it will conduct a trial itself, or remand the case for adjudication to the diocese that submitted it, along with appropriate procedural norms for processing the case. The bishop may also have requested that the priest be dismissed from the priesthood, *ex officio*. This process by which the cleric is immediately removed administratively by the pope is rarely utilized and only

for very serious cases. The Holy Father himself decides the case for immediate removal. There is no appeal or recourse. Ordinarily the cleric is invited to first seek for himself a dispensation from priestly obligations.

A recent development is the issue of prescription (a concept similar to the civil law "statute of limitation"). Although by prescription a person can bring a case of sexual abuse by a minor for action up until ten years from the victim's eighteenth birthday, the new procedural norms permit the waiving of this time limit by the Congregation for suitable reasons presented by the bishop.

Canonical Trial

The procedures for a canonical trial may be found in various sections of the *Code of Canon Law*:

Preliminary investigation: CIC 1717–1731 / CCEO 1468–1485

Trials in general: CIC 1400–1500 / CCEO 1055–1184

Contentious trials: CIC 1501–1670 / CCEO 1185–1356

Application of penalties: CIC 1341–1353 / CCEO 1468–1487

There have also been recent procedural changes made by the Congregation for the Doctrine of the Faith. The following is a brief outline of the penal procedure as conducted at a local diocese for the possible dismissal of a cleric from the clerical state.

1. The Promoter of Justice (PJ), a kind of ecclesiastical "district attorney" (or "prosecutor") presents a *libellus*. This is a report which asks the bishop to begin a case and lays out the case against the alleged offender. It will be the responsibility of the PJ to prove that the accused acted

with full knowledge and freedom in committing the crime (CIC 1721 / CCEO 1472).

2. In the case of a crime that might entail the penalty of dismissal from the clerical state, at least three judges must be appointed by the bishop. The new Roman instruction states that judges in these cases must be priests, although the Congregation may dispense this requirement (CIC 1425 §1, 2° / CCEO 1090 §2).

3. The accused must be formally cited and be invited to appoint an advocate within a time limit set by the judge. If one is not selected by the accused, a judge, under penalty of an invalid sentence, must appoint one. The right of defense is an important element in the penal process, and steps must be taken to assure a fair hearing CIC 1723 / CCEO 1474).

4. Then, the "joinder of the issues" takes place. In this part of the process, the judges determine the terms of the controversy, the grounds upon which the case will be examined. The purpose of the joinder of issues is to give precision to the focus of the proceedings, exactly establishing what will be alleged and proven to the satisfaction of the judges (CIC 1513 §1 / CCEO 1195).

5. In order to "prevent scandals, to protect the freedom of witnesses, and to guard the course of justice," the ordinary may impose restrictions on the ministry of the accused (e.g., exclude him from ministry) after the citation of the accused and hearing the PJ. The purpose of taking such steps is to protect the common good, the community, from any possible harm while the trial takes place. However, the diocesan bishop/eparch in accordance with the *Essential Norms*, has the latitude to use his executive power of governance at any time to make restrictions on the exercise of ministry of a suspect cleric. The accused has the right to appeal any such restrictions (see Chapter 6). They are to be rescinded when it is

apparent to the ordinary that they are no longer needed, or when the penal process is completed (CIC 1722 / CCEO 1473).

Presentation of Proof

6. Various types of proof can be submitted by the parties and by the judge, *ex officio* (CIC 1526–1586 / CCEO 1207–1271):

Declarations of parties: The judge may question the PJ and the accused in an effort to discover the truth in the case. He must question one of the parties when requested by the other party or to prove a fact which the public interest requires be proven beyond a reasonable doubt.

Documents: Both public church and civil documents may be produced. In the case of a trial to establish the commission of sexual abuse, the rulings of civil court, police, or government records could be submitted.

Witnesses: These can be an important source of evidence in a trial. A basic principle of canon law is that anyone not excluded by law can serve as a witness. Those exempted (but not necessarily excluded) include:

- Clerics, if what they would testify about was revealed to them by reason of their ministry (clerics are disqualified to testify concerning any matter learned through a sacramental confession)
- Civil officials
- Physicians
- Advocates
- Others bound by professional secrecy that relates to the case
- In addition, those who might expect to suffer some serious harm as a result of testifying are likewise exempted

Experts (e.g., psychiatrists, psychologists): It may be appropriate to involve experts who can help establish some fact or discern the true nature of a matter involved in the trial. It is up to the judge to appoint experts after consulting with the parties. It is also the responsibility of the judge to admit into evidence reports of experts that have already been assembled and are now presented to the court. It must be kept in mind, however, that although the experts may present helpful information and proof, the decision as to the establishment of guilt or innocence remains solely that of the judge(s).

Judicial examination and inspection: The judge may determine that it would be helpful to the case if he visited personally some place or inspected some things outside of the courtroom. For example, it may be appropriate to go to the place where the alleged sexual offenses occurred to see if the physical situation supports or does not support the claims of fact of the accuser(s). When the visit and/or inspection is completed, a report is to be prepared.

Presumptions: a presumption is a probable conjecture about an uncertain matter; a presumption in law is one the law itself establishes. For example, when an action is committed by a person, that person is presumed responsible for his or her action (CIC 1321, CCEO 1414).

The accused cannot be made to incriminate himself by confessing a crime. It is the responsibility of the PJ to prove that the delict has been committed (CIC 1728 §2, CCEO 1471).

7. The PJ may drop the case with the consent of the ordinary and agreement of accused (unless the accused was absent from the trial). If it becomes clear during the course of the proceedings that the case cannot be proven, the PJ may wish to abandon the case. Not only is the ordinary's consent who initiated the trial needed, but the accused must also agree. It may be that the person accused desires to protect his reputation and wishes to establish through the trial proceedings his innocence (CIC 1724, CCEO 1475).

If at any time of the penal trial it becomes evident to the judge(s) in virtue of the proofs or other acts of the case, that the defendant is innocent, the judge must declare this in a sentence and absolve the accused (CIC 1726, CCEO 1482).

Decision

8. The accused (or the advocate of the accused) has the right to the last word after the discussion of the case, prior to the decision. It is the law's desire, in an effort to protect the right of self-defense, to allow the accused (or his advocate) to have the opportunity to write or speak last, just before the decision is rendered (CIC 1725, CCEO 1478).

9. Decisions can take several forms:

   ◆ The judges' sentence may declare the accused innocent of the charge.

   ◆ The judges may declare in their sentence *non constat*, the delict has not been proven with moral certitude, beyond a reasonable doubt (not quite as strong as establishing the complete innocence of the accused).

   ◆ The judges may find that the offense is not actionable, e.g., the person who claims to have been sexually abused by a cleric was not a minor according to the law that was in effect at the time the alleged crime was committed.

   ◆ Or the judges may give an affirmative decision, *constat*, that the crime has indeed been proven and that a penalty is warranted (CIC 1726, CCEO 1482).

10. Just penalties, including the possible dismissal from the clerical state, are required for sexual abuse of a minor by a cleric. The "just penalties" mentioned could include a variety of serious restrictions on the ministry of the offending cleric (CIC 1336, CCEO 1432). The judges have some discretionary powers, including the postponement

of the penalty for compelling reasons (CIC 1395 §2, CCEO 1453 §1).

11. In the case of an affirmative decision, the accused may choose to appeal to the Congregation for the Doctrine of the Faith. Likewise in the case of a negative decision, the PJ may also choose to challenge the sentence. The PJ may also choose to appeal if it is believed that the repair of scandal or restoration of justice has not been sufficiently provided for (CIC 1727, CCEO 1481). The appeal suspends the execution of the sentence (CIC 1353, CCEO 1319).

After a decision, the acts are always to be transmitted to the Congregation for the Doctrine of the Faith.

Apostolic Signatura: the supreme tribunal of the Catholic Church.

Arbitration: the hearing and determining of a dispute between parties by a person chosen by the parties themselves. Normally the determination and outcome is left to the discretion of the arbiter by agreement of the parties.

Associations of the Christian faithful: a group of the Christian faithful organized for spiritual, charitable, or apostolic works.

Charter for the Protection of Children and Young People: document of the USCCB, committing the bishops to actively and promptly respond to allegations of sexual misconduct by clergy. The Charter was accompanied by *Essential Norms* detailing the procedure by which allegations would be reviewed and prosecuted.

Christian faithful: those incorporated into Christ through baptism and constituted as the "People of God."

Code of Canon Law: a systematic arrangement of the laws of the Roman Catholic Church which occurred during the pontificate of Pope Pius X, promulgated by his successor, Pope Benedict XV in 1917. Pope John Paul II promulgated a new Code in 1983. It applies primarily to Catholics of the Latin Rite.

Code of Canons of Eastern Churches: body of laws promulgated for the twenty-one Eastern autonomous churches who have their own hierarchy and are in communion with the bishop of Rome.

Conciliation: informal process in which a third party tries to bring disagreeing parties to some agreement.

Due Process: effort to peaceably resolve a dispute between parties in disagreement, as an alternative to litigation.

Eparch: equivalent term in the Eastern church for a diocesan bishop in the Latin church.

Eparchy: equivalent term in the Eastern church for a diocese in the Latin church.

Executive Power: power of governance exercised by a Church official, normally a bishop.

Hierarchic Recourse: formal canonical procedure of appeal, asking for the revocation or amendment of an administrative act of the bishop, made to his hierarchical superior.

Holy See (Apostolic See): a term that applies not only to the pope but also to the Secretariat of State and other offices of the Roman Curia.

Lex Ecclesiae Fundamentalis: an effort made by the Commission for the Revision of the *Code of Canon Law* to formulate a "fundamental law of the Church." Many of the rights drafted in this document have been included in the 1983 code.

Peace on Earth (*Pacem in Terris*): an encyclical issued by Pope John XXIII on April 11, 1963, within the context of escalating tensions in international relations. It was addressed to "all people of good will" and offered the services of the Catholic Church in helping to relieve cold war tensions with gospel values and the assertion of human rights for all people.

Promoter of Justice: a court official appointed by the bishop for the protection of the public good. The Promoter acts somewhat analogously to a public defender in an ecclesiastical penal trial.

Recognitio: formal recognition by the appropriate Roman office, permitting particular norms of an episcopal conference to become effective for its territory.

The Condition of Labor (*Rerum Novarum*): groundbreaking encyclical of Pope Leo XIII, often identified as a landmark for Catholic social teaching. Issued on May 15, 1891, it was written to address a myriad of social problems of the age, including questions about labor unions, the dignity of the worker, and the need for better working conditions.

Review Board: part of the process outlined by the Dallas charter and *Essential Norms* in pursuing cases of possible sexual misconduct by a cleric; this group of at least five persons of "outstanding integrity and good judgment" functions as a consultative body to the bishop in discharging his responsibilities in reviewing cases of allegations of the abuse of a minor by a cleric.

Safeguarding of the Sanctity of the Sacraments (*Sacramentorum Sanctitatis Tutela*): document promulgated by Pope John Paul II, April 30, 2001, concerning procedures to be followed when certain grave, ecclesiastical crimes are alleged, including the sexual abuse of a minor by a cleric.

United States Conference of Catholic Bishops (USCCB): the organization of the U.S. hierarchy, functioning as the episcopal conference of the United States, empowered to make policy, subject to review by the Holy See.

Sources and Recommended Readings

Abbot, W., gen. ed., *The Documents of Vatican II*, New York: Guild Press, 1966.

Beal, J., J. Coriden, and T. Green, *New Commentary on the Code of Canon Law*, New York: Paulist Press, 2000.

Brundage, T., "Canonical Issues in Due Process" in *CLSA Proceedings* 63(2001), 37–48.

———., "Resolving Disputes Within the Church" in *America*, Oct. 29, 2001, 20–21.

———., "The Rights of Priests in the Code of Canon Law," in *The Priest*, January 1994, 13–18.

Canon Law Society of America, *Code of Canon Law: Latin English Translation*, Washington, D.C.: CLSA, 1999.

———., *Code of Canons of the Eastern Churches: Latin-English Translation*, Washington, D.C.: CLSA, 2001.

———., *Revised Guide to the Implementation of the U.S. Bishops Essential Norms for Diocesan/Epurchial Policies Dealing With Allegations of Sexual Abuse of Minors by Priests or Deacons*, Washington, D.C.: CLSA, 2004.

Caparros, E. and M. Theriault, eds., *Code of Canon Law Annotated*, Montreal: Wilson & Lafleur, 1993.

Coriden, J., "A Challenge: Making the Rights Real," in *The Jurist*, 45(1985), 1–23.

Coriden J., T. Green and D. Heintschel, *The Code of Canon Law: A Text and Commentary*, New York: Paulist Press, 1985.

McKenna, K., "The Clergy's Right of Confidentiality" in *The Priest*, November 1991, 37–50.

———., *A Concise Guide to Catholic Social Teaching*, Notre Dame: Ave Maria Press, 2002.

————., "The Dallas Charter and Due Process" in *America,* September 16, 2002, 7–11.

————., *The Ministry of Law in the Church Today,* Notre Dame: University of Notre Dame Press, 1998.

————., "Psychological Screening for Religious Life" in *Review for Religious,* 54, No. 4, 589–593.

————., "The Revised Essential Norms and Some Lingering Concerns" in *Touchstone, National Federation of Priests' Councils,* Winter, 2002, 12–13.

Morrisey, F., "Denial of Access to the Sacraments" in *CLSA Proceedings* 52(1990), 170–186.

Provost, J., "Ecclesial Rights," in *CLSA Proceedings* 44(1982), 41–62.

United States Conference of Catholic Bishops, *Promise to Protect, Pledge to Heal: Charter for the Protection of Children and Young People, Essential Norms, Statement of Episcopal Commitment,* Washington, D.C.: USCCB, 2002.

ℐndex

Rev. Kevin E. McKenna is the pastor of St. Cecilia Parish in Rochester, New York, and General Editor of the Concise Guide Series from Ave Maria Press. Ordained in 1977, he received his doctoral degree in canon law from St. Paul University in Ottawa in 1990. Fr. McKenna served as chancellor of the Diocese of Rochester from 1992–2001 and president of the Canon Law Society of America from 2001–2002.

Fr. McKenna is the author of numerous articles on Church law and ministry and of four previous books:

The Ministry of Law in the Church Today (University of Notre Dame Press)

A Concise Guide to Canon Law (Ave Maria Press)

A Concise Guide to Catholic Social Teaching (Ave Maria Press)

You Did It For Me: Care of Your Neighbor as a Spiritual Practice (Ave Maria Press)